The Hitler Trophy

Floodlit Dreams

The Hitler Trophy

Golf and the Olympic Games

By Alan Fraser

Published by Floodlit Dreams Ltd, 2016.

A CIP catalogue record for this book is available from the British Library.

ISBN 978-0-9926585-5-7

Floodlit Dreams Ltd
5-6 George St
St Albans
Herts AL3 4ER.

www.floodlitdreams.com

Cover design by Mike McMonagle
Plate section edited by Alex Ridley
Typeset by Peloton Publishing

To my lovely Morag

THE HITLER TROPHY
CONTENTS

1

LOT 169

Lot 169 of the Bonhams Sporting and Golfing Memorabilia Auction held in Chester, England on the 29th of May, 2012, had attracted a considerable amount of interest.

The inside cover of the glossy catalogue revealed a full-page colour photograph of a silver-gilt salver which appeared to be decorated with a circular inlay of eight tinned peaches. At least that was the impression given by the strange yellow panels.

The Claret Jug, it was not. It would take the most generous of beholders to see beauty in this odd trophy.

The 'yellow peaches', two and a half inches in diameter, were, in fact, amber, a one-time popular German stone found on the shores of the Baltic Sea. A stamp of the letter 'L' identified the maker as the famous Berlin Court goldsmith Emil Lettre who operated from prestigious workshops in Unter-den-Linden.

The hand of Lettre was, however, neither the main selling point nor the reason for the buzz surrounding Lot 169 in the New House saleroom that last Tuesday in May.

'GOLFPREIS der NATIONEN,' the trophy declared.

'GEGEBEN VOM FUHRER und REICHSKANZLER.'

You would need little or no knowledge of the German language to work out that this was an international golf prize donated by none other than Adolf Hitler. A unique golf prize, moreover. Unique because Hitler (a painter not a golfer – "two coats, one afternoon," according to demented Nazi lover Franz Liebkind

9

in that wonderful film The Producers) was not in the habit of commissioning trophies for any sporting event, never mind golf. Unique because the trophy was contested, won and presented only the once, at Baden-Baden Golf Club in late August, 1936.

The year and the timing are significant. The international team competition was staged deliberately as a postscript to the notorious 1936 Berlin Olympic Games. Although golf had not been included among the events of the Olympiad there is overwhelming evidence that the German hosts afforded the event quasi-Olympic status and that the participants themselves felt they were taking part in the Games.

The trophy was won by England – not Great Britain – represented by the Yorkshire/Lancashire, white rose/red rose combination of Tom Thirsk and Arnold Bentley.

The reaction of the Germans, who had led at the half-way stage of the two-day, four-round event and had begun to entertain thoughts of an unlikely victory, varied between disappointment and fury, depending on their understanding of the world's golfing hierarchy. Hitler, for example, who was to golf what Tiger Woods is to painting, was said to be incandescent. The trophy, after all, bore his title if not his actual name.

As it transpired, the English Golf Union, no doubt prompted by hindsight, grew less and less thrilled at having been presented with the trophy by their nominated troops, Thirsk and Bentley.

The EGU were to 'give it away' in the 1950s, the start of a journey which saw the trophy move from one home to another, spending time on the bar of a London club and 'being lost' only to turn up in a large detached house on the outskirts of Glasgow.

Once 'found', having also spent time in the British Golf Museum in St Andrews, the distinctive trophy was to come under the hammer.

Dotted around the room in Chester that day, among the usual collectors of sporting memorabilia, could be spotted two representatives from a well-known Lancashire Golf Club, a prominent member from a Yorkshire club and a mysterious German gentleman.

Unknown to all of them, another person interested in what had now become known as The Hitler Trophy had left commission bids on the book.

As the auctioneer invited bids for Lot 169 another chapter opened on an Olympic golf story which began in Paris in 1900 and was to enter a new phase in Rio de Janeiro in 2016.

2

HOW TO WIN AN OLYMPIC
GOLD MEDAL AND NOT KNOW IT

It could be argued that the international golf tournament at Baden-Baden in 1936 was every bit as much a part of Olympic history as the golf event held at Compiègne in 1900. Which is not saying a great deal.

Both would have taken place under the radar, had it been invented. The only difference was that the International Olympic Committee recognised one and not the other.

Yet, most competitors turning up for the golf competition at Compiègne Golf Club 50 miles north of the centre of Paris at the start of the 20th century had not the faintest idea that they were taking part in the Olympic Games. Those same competitors departed equally unaware that they had played in the first Olympic golf event.

Indeed, somewhat bizarrely, though almost understandably when one considers the chaotic nature of the organisation, Peggy Abbott, the women's golf champion, died in 1955 still ignorant of the fact that she had been an Olympian and oblivious to her status as the first American woman to win an Olympic gold medal. Britain's Charlotte Cooper, the Wimbledon champion in 1895 and 1896, similarly had no idea that when winning the tennis event on the Ile de Puteaux courts in July she became the first woman to win an Olympic gold medal.

As far as Abbott was concerned, having read an advertisement in a Parisian newspaper, she was entering a nine-hole amateur event for the championship of Paris. She would have considered her subsequent October victory in the French women's championship at Dinard on the Brittany coast much more important. Thinking the Compiègne occasion might be a fun day out, she urged her Parisian friends and fellow socialites to come along. The French women seemed to regard the occasion as an opportunity to display their latest wears. According to one contemporary newspaper report, they 'apparently misunderstood the nature of the game scheduled for that day and turned up to play in high heels and tight skirts.'

A report in the *New York Herald* the week prior to the start of the golf spoke of an age now long gone. 'Most of the visitors,' it reported, 'have made arrangements to stay over at Compiègne on Tuesday night when there will be a dance and cotillion in the club room.' Helpfully, the same article provided information on the times of trains to and from Paris.

The modern Olympic era had begun four years earlier in Athens. Unlike 1900, no one in the Greek capital or beyond was in any doubt about what was happening. Bunting adorned every public building; the initials OA (the Greek initials of the Olympic Games) and the dates on the banners, BC 776 and AD 1896, signified the start of the Ancient Games and its rebirth in modern form; opening and closing ceremonies gave structure to the nine-day event; with the unavailability of the Olympic Stadium, which was pretty much in ruins, the Panathenaic Stadium, built in 330 BC and restored painstakingly using white marble, provided a magnificent centrepiece for the occasion.

A new running track was prepared by Charles Perry, the groundsman at Stamford Bridge (the football stadium not the battle) would you believe. Contrary to modern practice, the track raced clockwise and included a turn so tight that athletes were forced to slow down almost to walking pace when negotiating it.

The swimming venue was no more than a pier in the sea near

Piraeus. So rough were the conditions there that the sailing and rowing events had to be cancelled. But the 1200 metre swim took place with the winner, Alfred Hajos of Hungary, later confessing: 'My will to live completely overcame my desire to win.' It was deemed fortunate that no-one did drown.

It is difficult to be accurate about figures since different sources quote different numbers. But the best authority suggests that 241 (all male) athletes from 14 countries competed in 43 separate events covering nine sporting disciplines. About two thirds represented the host nation. Contrast that with the figures for Athens 2004 – 10,625 athletes (6,296 men and 4,329 women), 201 nations, 301 events, 28 disciplines - and one can see immediately the size of the Olympic beast created.

There might have been a few more back in 1896, especially from the United States, but for the tack taken by one *New York Times* editorial. 'The American amateur sportsman in general should know that in going to Athens he is taking an expensive journey to a third rate capital where he will be devoured by fleas.'

Track and field dominated, then as now, with cycling, fencing, artistic gymnastics, shooting, swimming, tennis, weightlifting and Greco-Roman wrestling completing the schedule. There was no golf, not least because there were no golf courses in Greece. Even today, there are only a handful.

Paris at the turn of the century was the playground of the west. The Metro opened its first few stations in July 1900; Sacre Coeur was growing out of the remnants of the Commune's last stand. And the Olympic Games provided a perfect opportunity to showcase the French capital.

Or did it? Paris 1900, though involving 997 athletes from 24 countries according to official IOC figures, amounted to little more than a sideshow of the World Exhibition. Pierre, Baron de Coubertin, the founder of the modern Olympics, had expected to be in control of his hometown games. But the French government took over while giving every indication they knew not what they were staging. Hence the somewhat clumsy official title, Concours Internationaux d'Exercises Physiques et de Sport – in English, the International Meeting of Physical Exercises and Sport – further evidence for those who consider the Paris sporting contests to have become the second modern Olympiad only retrospectively in order to maintain the four-year cycle.

Ludicrously, the events spanned five months and suffered from a lamentable lack of organisation and marketing. The Games began with fencing in June and ended with golf in October. Venues, often totally unsuitable and anything but purpose-built, were spread far and wide.

Contrast the Panathenaic Stadium with the sodden, bumpy running surface at Croix-Catelan in the Bois de Boulogne provided by the French for the supposedly high profile track and field. There was, in actual fact, no track and just a field.

Hurdles were erected using broken telephone poles; long jumpers were required to dig their own pits. The discus frequently flew into the crowd which stood around the perimeter in the absence of any grandstands. There were reports of hammers catching in the trees like golf drivers thrown in anger. Come on, we have all done it.

The swimming, meanwhile, was held in the River Seine with strong currents that either hurtled swimmers down the river at inflated speeds or pretty much prevented them from getting anywhere. As if to prove there's nowt stranger than the French, the swimming included an underwater race and an obstacle race in which the contestants climbed over – and swam under – chained rowing boats.

Given that these Games, like those of 1904 in St Louis, were attached to the World Exhibition, there existed the utterly bizarre situations whereby the fencing was part of the 'Cutlery Exhibition' and the rowing was included in 'Life-Saving'. Don't ask for an explanation.

Journalists were few and spectators only marginally more numerous, principally because organisers failed to publicise times and venues. Prospective competitors were left similarly in the dark. The biggest attendance was recorded for the October final of the rugby union, in which France thrashed Great Britain.

Disorganised chaos prevailed. Take the case of the discus champion, Rudolf Bauer of Hungary, who stood proudly at the top of the podium only for the Stars and Stripes to be raised to the unmistakeable strains of the American anthem. Bauer objected. The ceremony was halted only to resume with the correct Hungarian flag being hoisted against a background of the Austrian national anthem. Never mind God Bless America, God bless France.

No medals were awarded. They were struck many years later by the IOC and awarded posthumously. The champions of 1900 instead received more mundane prizes such as books and umbrellas. Peggy Abbott was presented with a Saxon porcelain bowl decorated in chiselled gold.

The women's golf event attracted just 10 entries, five French and five Americans, though even a century later it is not possible to be precise about nationality. Time has revealed, for example that 'Polly' Whittier, originally said to be from Switzerland, was, in fact, Pauline Whittier of Boston, a descendant of the poet John Greenleaf Whittier. In 1900 she was studying at St Moritz. Mrs J Huger Pratt, meanwhile, entered out of Dinard in France, was the former Daria Parkhurst who, scandal of scandals, divorced before marrying Prince Alexis Karageorgevitch of Serbia.

Margaret Abbott, to give her the name on her birth certificate, was born in India in 1878, the daughter of the celebrated novelist Mary Perkins Ives Abbott. The family spent five years in Calcutta where Peggy's father worked as a merchant. Her mother published her first novel, Alexia, in 1889 to be followed in 1890 by The Beverleys: A Story of Calcutta.

On being widowed, Mary Abbott, from Salem just outside Boston, moved to Chicago to be near her brother, a railroad official. Mary was a journalist as well as an author, an arts editor and regular book reviewer with the *Chicago Tribune* and *Chicago Evening Post*. She established a literary salon dedicated to encouraging young Chicago writers and became a great favourite of the city's old money who would attend conversational gatherings at her apartment.

A colleague at that time was Finley Peter Dunne. Dunne's most celebrated creation was Mr Dooley, a south side Chicago publican who appeared in satirical sketches sometimes read aloud at the cabinet of President Theodore Roosevelt. But Dunne's remarkable range spread across the entire spectrum of journalism from political reporter, a columnist writing on subjects as diverse as astronomy, music and aviation, editorial writer and managing editor to a humble sports reporter covering the Chicago White Sox.

Miss Abbott, boasting a golfing pedigree unmatched by any of her adversaries, teed off at Compiègne as the strong favourite. Peggy and her mother, Mary, had taken up golf in 1897 at the prestigious Chicago Golf Club in Wheaton, Illinois, under the tutelage of Charles Blair McDonald, the so-called father of American golf.

MacDonald, the first winner of the US Amateur Championship, was a bull of a man with a physique, according to his many detractors, dwarfed by the size of his ego. Born in Chicago, he had been sent by his father at the age of 16 to continue his education at the United Colleges of St Salvator and St Leonard in Scotland.

There he discovered golf. He was fortunate indeed to develop his game in the company of players of the stature of Young Tom Morris, the finest golfer of his generation, and Davy Strath whose name lives on in the notorious cavernous bunker guarding the front of the 11th green at the Old Course in St Andrews.

MacDonald returned to the States as golf's greatest advocate.

17

His zeal in attempting to convert his friends to the 'Scottish game', as it was known over there, extended to ordering six sets of clubs from Liverpool and having them shipped on board the ocean liner The Majestic. Not content with having laid out holes in Lake Forest, leading to the formation of the Onwentsia Club, he decided to pass round the hat among 30 of his friends asking for 10 dollars each towards the building of a new course on the stock farm of a Musselburgh man, A Haddon Smith. This course at Belmont, 25 miles from Chicago and easily accessible by train (an important factor in the development of golf wherever it was played at the time), became the prestigious Chicago Golf Club.

The membership may have comprised those and such as those but there was nothing fancy about the amenities. There was, for example, no clubhouse with players reduced to storing clubs in a neighbouring barn.

The number of members grew, however, as did the need to expand. A 200 acre farm was acquired in Dupage County, 25 miles from Wheaton, the location of the Chicago Golf Club to this day. Macdonald would glory in his nickname, the Laird of Wheaton.

Competitive sport in America at this time remained very much the preserve of the social elite. The upper class used their free time and their largely old inherited money to avail themselves of a variety of recreational options provided by the likes of yachting, horse racing, lawn tennis and increasingly golf. The burgeoning railway system allowed city slickers to feed their fascination for English country life.

Not everyone was welcome, however. Chicago's population may have been 30% German but prosperous German American Jews were barred from membership at the exclusive Midwest golf clubs. Four decades later, Hitler was to order the expulsion of Jews from all German golf clubs.

Peggy Abbott, fierce and charming in both competition and life, had won several local and regional competitions at home in

Chicago prior to heading to France with her mother in 1899. In Paris, the 22-year-old socialite and aspiring painter, studied art under the likes of Edgar Degas and Auguste Rodin at a time when Claude Monet was introducing impressionism to an eager world. For physical recreation she would play the occasional round of golf with the American ex-pat community.

The following summer on July 18, several months prior to the Olympic golf event, the *New York Times* repeated an item published the previous day in a Chicago newspaper. It read: 'social circles here (Chicago) are in a flutter over the announcement of the engagement of Miss Margaret Abbott of this city to Pierre Deschamps of Paris.'

This turned out to be the same Pierre Deschamps who in creating the French Golf Federation became known as the 'father of French golf'. (Peggy seemed to like her golfing 'fathers'.) A brilliant student and later diplomat, Deschamps progressed through the corps to first secretary to the ambassador in St Petersburg. It is thought that the couple probably met in 1897 at the golf club in Chicago. That was where Deschamps – in much the same way as the young Peggy Abbott – discovered golf.

But the engagement did not translate into a wedding. The next we hear about Miss Abbott's romantic adventures is her marriage to the aforementioned Finley Dunne on December 10, 1902. The glamorous couple were to have two children, one of whom made a significant mark on the film industry. Philip Ives Dunne (born 1908, died 1992) became a Hollywood screenwriter, director and producer whose film credits included *The Last of the Mohicans* (1936), *How Green Was My Valley* (1941) and *The Robe* (1953).

Philip Dunne, together with celebrated directors William Wyler and John Huston, formed the Committee for the First Amendment to protect against the procedures of the House Un-American Activities Committee. Dunne also headed the Motion Picture Bureau of the Office of War Information during World

19

War II before going on to become a founding member of the American Screen Writer's Guild. Meanwhile, he and his wife's bluff-top Malibu home served as a social and political Mecca for Hollywood's liberal community and as a think tank for vocal opponents of first McCarthyism and then the Vietnam war.

The first Olympic Ladies Golf Championship was held on October 2, 1900. Peggy Abbott, who was reported as having completed the nine holes during practice in 36, managed only a 47 on the big day by virtue of some shoddy work on and around the greens. But that proved plenty good enough for a two-stroke victory over the aforementioned Polly Whittier. Abbott's mother finished seventh, 18 strokes behind her daughter, with the unfortunate Madame Brun of the local club crashing – in modern tabloid parlance – to a disastrous 80, no doubt encumbered by the tightest of skirts and the pointiest of high heels.

Final scores were:

47 - Miss M Abbott (Chicago GC); **49** - Miss P Whittier (St Moritz GC); **53** - Mrs Huger Pratt (Dinard GC), Mme Froment-Maurice (Compiègne); **57** - Mrs Bridgway (Deauville Golf Club); **64** - Mme Fourmier-Sartoveze (Compiègne); **65** - Mrs Abbott (Chicago GC), Caronne Fain (Compiègne); **76** - Mme Gelbert (Compiègne); **80** - Mme Brun (Compiègne).

The *New York Herald* passed favourable judgement on the gold medallist: "The chief feature of Miss Abbott's game is her driving and brassie play, her style being perfect. Her tall, supple figure allows her to bring her club onto the ball with a beautiful free body swing, and it rarely happens that she makes a bad stroke." Sadly, arthritis was to end her golf when in her 60s.

The same American newspaper, who noted that Abbott was a great favourite among ex-pat society in Paris, lavished praise on both the venue and an occasion pretty much ignored by the British press, a couple of golf magazines excepted.

"The enthusiastic followers of the Royal and Ancient game

who came to Compiègne for the first time were indeed astonished to find such an admirable 18-hole course and such perfect arrangements," the *New York Herald* enthused. "It can only be regretted that the distance from the metropolis prevents Parisians from patronizing these links on a larger scale. Every foot of the turf on the greens had to be specially laid down. It is doubtful whether better ones can be found on any other continental enclosure. Naturally, the lack of rain had rendered the greens rather fast.

"The links is of good average length. Most of the holes are well guarded by numerous bunkers, high trees and nasty little bushes, not to speak of the long grass on and near the racecourse. The entries obtained were very satisfactory, although one cannot help being sorry that more of the crack English and Scotch (sic) players were not present."

The newspaper said of the men's event: "The best and most experienced exponent of the game competing was Mr W Rutherford of the Jedburgh GC who has for years enjoyed the advantage of playing at St Andrews and on other noble links in Scotland with some of the very best players of the day."

Of Walter Rutherford, little is known. A handicap of plus 2, by far the lowest in the event, confirmed his stature as the most accomplished player participating. One report suggested that a late arrival and a lack of practice might explain his having to settle for the silver medal, a single stroke behind the champion, Charles Sands, a three handicapper, from the St Andrews GC at Yonkers, New York.

We know that Rutherford was born a son of the manse in 1936 at Newlands in the Scottish borders and that he died aged 66 in Westminster, London. We know, too, that he was a good enough to win the Borders Golfers' Association title. And that is about it. There was some suggestion that he had been a grain merchant who fell on bad times.

21

More is known about his fellow Scot David Donaldson Robertson who won the bronze medal, albeit a distant seven strokes behind the runner up. Robertson packed a great deal into the 68 years of a life that began in the affluent Shawlands area of Glasgow and ended in Royal Berkshire in 1937.

He was born into wealth and position. His father, William Alexander Robertson, described as a wine merchant on his son's birth certificate, was to become one of the pioneers of the Scottish blended whisky industry. Robertson Snr. founded the historic Robertson & Baxter company in 1861 which in various guises – including a period of control by the noted philanthropists, the Robertson sisters, Elspeth, Agnes and Ethel – survived and thrived into the present day Edrington Group, distillers of such well known brands as The Macallan, Highland Park, The Famous Grouse and Cutty Sark.

David Robertson, the sixth of 12 to survive childbirth, began his education at Haileybury School in Hertfordshire, the alma mater of luminaries such as Clement Atlee, playwright Sir Alan Ayckbourn and the painter Rex Whistler. He continued his schooling at Glasgow Academy before progressing to university at first Glasgow then Christ's College, Cambridge. A speedy wing threequarter, Robertson played in the notorious 1892 Varsity Match which ended in a 0-0 draw in a mud bath at Queen's Club in London. It was while a student that he earned a solitary cap for Scotland, having been on the losing side against Wales at Murrayfield. He was one of six dropped after that 0-9 defeat and was never picked again.

Robertson was called to the bar at Lincoln's Inn in 1895, the start of a distinguished career which included a piece of legal work, as his grandson Anthony revealed, involving an event dear to the hearts of golfing people on both sides of the Atlantic.

"DD, as the family called him, drafted an agreement and drew up the deed for the Ryder Cup," Anthony recalled. "I knew he played a bit of golf but I had no idea until you told me that he played in the Olympic Games. I certainly know nothing about a bronze medal. There was one golfing story involving DD. He attended Cambridge and one of his brothers went to Oxford. They were both involved in one of the Varsity golf matches in the late 1800s. As I understand it, they were drawn against each other and it was decided to do a redraw because neither fancied playing his brother.

"The Robertsons know DD as a rugger player and a bloody good shot. He lived in Cheney Walk in Chelsea and had the fourth bank account at the Nat West in King's Road. That has proved useful for loans over the years! He was also a director of the London, Midland and Scotland (LMS) Railway Company.

"He met his wife on the touchline of a Scotland v England hockey match. His three sisters were playing for Scotland while the sister of his future wife was playing for England. Elsie (née Jackson) was a formidable woman. An engineer, she was involved in building the railway line over The Andes."

Robertson had entered the Olympic Games out of Northwood Golf Club, near London. Northwood exists today but has no record of their Olympian.

The men's champion, the American in Paris, recorded a score of 167 for 36 holes. Remarkably, Charles Sands had reached the final of the inaugural US Amateur Championship in 1895 just three months after taking up golf. That represented an astonishing achievement and never mind that he was walloped 12 and 11 by our old friend Charles B. MacDonald. That seemed to be enough for Sands who never entered the US Amateur a second time. It transpired that the Olympic victory represented his only golfing triumph.

Although a renowned all-round athlete, tennis was really his game. He was to become US champion in 1905 in court tennis, the original form of the game. Sands remains one of only a handful of American athletes to have competed in the Olympics in three sports – golf and lawn tennis in 1900 and jeu de paume (the original name for court tennis) in 1908.

The *New York Herald* introduced the champion to its readers thus: "Mr Sands has of late been practising hard on the links of the Paris Golf Club at Mesnil-le-Roi. He does not claim to be a golfer at all, although he got into the finals at Newport, Rhode Island, in 1895. His name is chiefly connected with tennis and lawn tennis and he holds the tennis (jeu de paume) championship of France.

"But he is one of those men who are good at any game they make their mind up to go in for, and his success was very popular. His golfing style is by no means perfect. His drive is not even a three quarter swing, but he puts a tremendous amount of power into the stroke. The chief feature of his game is his approaching and putting. He is most deadly on the green and runs down long putts with surprising regularity."

Somewhat bizarrely, the *Herald* correspondent took a couple of gentle swipes at the golfers and their followers.

"It must at once be said that the golfing community, like lawn tennis players and disciples of other branches of amateur sport, are by no means early birds," the reporter observed. "At Compiègne, the enjoyment of the morning hours is left to the 'pioupious' and 'citrouilles', as the infantry and cavalry soldiers of the Republic are familiarly called, of the local garrison. Your average golfer finds little charm in the rattle of the drums or the bugle calls which sound the soldiers' reveille. In nine cases out of 10 he prefers to lie in bed and dream lazily of lofty drives, brilliant putts, and record rounds. The pity of it!

"…All the inhabitants of Compiègne seemed to have turned out in force to watch 'le golf'. But, alas, they were a noisy lot, and continued conversing even at the most critical moments. No wonder that many a drive was 'foozled' and many a putt missed."

Golf Illustrated, the influential British magazine, seemed in its infancy more interested in the social side of things. The writer penned the following: "The International Golf Competition recently held at Compiègne in connection with the Paris Exhibition, seems to have been quite a success. The entries were numerous, the play good, the weather admirable and the company (by which I mean spectators, officials and others connected with or responsible for the meeting) distinguished and enthusiastic. Amongst those present were Prince and Princess R du Lucinge, Madama Vagliano, Comte and Comtesse Robert de Breda, Vicomte and Vicomtesse d'Hautpoul, Comte and Comtesse de Moussac, General and Miss French, M and Mme Saint-Olive, M Dutilleul, Comte and Comtesse d'Orsetti, Mme Delagarde, Lt Jaubert and M de Luze and Lord Sudeley.

"In connection with the Tournament, a luncheon banquet was held in a large marquee, and in the evening a big dinner was given by the Compiègne Club, followed by a dance, in the Hotel de la Cloche. For the success of the function as a whole much credit is due to Comte Jacques du Pourtales (chief steward) and Lt Fournier-Sarloveze."

It was left to the *St Louis Globe-Democrat* to make passing reference to an intriguing incident which occurred in the men's handicap event, a secondary competition subsequently not afforded Olympic status.

"(Mackenzie)Turpie, who paid his own entry fee and expenses purely for the honour of competing, is a postman at St Andrews, Scotland," the paper reported.

"Sundry of the visitors objected to a postman playing in their company. Count Fourtales and Lieutenant Safflovezo, the stewards of the tournament, decided that in republican France a postman was the equal of a peer. Turpie was entitled to play as an amateur golfer in their opinion irrespective of what his occupation might be."

The *Herald*, meanwhile, reported that 'four players tied on the 80 mark, among them being a Scotchman, Mr Mackenzie Turpie, who had come all the way from St Andrews. He had the satisfaction of winning the fifth medal on playing off the tie and would no doubt have done much better if he had had time for a preliminary round or two."

Sadly, no record of (seven handicap) 'Turpie' could be found among the various St Andrews clubs and the local newspapers of the era. The 1911 Census, however, reveals a McKenzie Turpie (49), a postman, living with his wife, Margaret, at 118 North Street in St Andrews. The same McKenzie Turpie died from a heart attack on 15th October, 1930.

The handicap event was won by millionaire Albert Bond Lambert, the president of the manufacturers of Listerine after whom the present-day international airport in St Louis is named. And Lambert was to be an influential figure in the 1904 Olympic Games held in his home town of St Louis.

3

MEET ME ON THE FIRST TEE
IN ST LOUIS

Albert Bond Lambert – "a nice young man, one of the nicest anyone would know, and he is a good golfer," the *St Louis Globe-Democrat* reported – was responsible for, metaphorically speaking, carrying the golfing baton from Paris, France to St Louis, USA and between the Olympic Games of 1900 and 1904.

Lambert, the president of Lambert Pharmaceutical, later to become Warner-Lambert and more recently part of the Pfizer empire, had travelled to the World Fair in Paris at the turn of the century primarily to promote and market his company's latest product, Listerine, to this day the most enduring and best known of mouthwashes. The same Lambert, an even more avid aviator than golfer, signed up enthusiastically to be a benefactor for Charles Lindbergh's first solo transatlantic flight from New York to Paris on the Spirit of St Louis in 1927. The Lambert-St Louis International Airport still bears his name.

While in France, Lambert took time off to participate in the international event handicap division, not subsequently officially recognised by the IOC. An 83, less a 10 handicap, proved sufficient for a victory which fired his enthusiasm for the Olympic experience. He could not wait to return home to St Louis where he regaled his father-in-law Colonel George McGrew with tales of his French experience.

Now his wife's Dad just happened to be the founder member of Glen Echo Golf Club in St Louis. McGrew, in fact, had established Mound City Club, as Glen Echo was originally named, after travelling to St Andrews and becoming enthralled with the game while playing in the company of Old Tom Morris, no less. Back in Missouri, McGrew purchased 167 acres of rolling farmland which was transformed into America's first 18-hole golf course west of the Mississippi River.

The design and construction had been entrusted to Scottish brothers, James and Robert Foulis, both pupils of the aforementioned Morris. James emigrated in 1895 to take up the position of head professional at the Chicago Golf Club. The following year he was to become US Open Champion. Glen Echo, situated 12 miles north west of St Louis (and, scarily, about a mile from the haunted home that inspired the 1973 film *The Exorcist*), presented narrow targets off the tee, rolling fairways and sloping greens.

Nowadays, it is touted as the oldest Olympic venue in continuous use. Visitors to Glen Echo can purchase a replica of an Olympic medal. Two flags flank the main entrance to the club – one is Old Glory, the other the Olympic standard of five coloured rings on a white background. An Olympic torch and various forms of memorabilia are scattered throughout the property.

"This is an Olympic site, a very special place," golf historian Jim Healey proclaimed to *Golf Digest* magazine in 2009.

But it might not have been. The third Olympiad had been bound for Chicago. Baron de Coubertin wanted it in the Midwest capital; President Teddy Roosevelt gave his backing to the Windy City; no sooner had the Paris Games finished than newspapers in the US were declaring that Chicago would host the next Olympics.

It seemed a fait accompli. That was until St Louis, America's fourth largest city at the time, threatened to run in opposition its own sports festival as part of the Louisiana Purchase Exposition. De Coubertin and Co took fright. Anxious that their Olympics might be regarded as secondary to the Exposition and, worse still, fail to make money because of the clash, the IOC voted overwhelmingly at an ad hoc session in Paris in December 1902 to switch to St Louis.

"Meet me in St Louis, Louis," the 1904 song went. "Meet me at the fair." And at the Olympic Games, as it transpired.

But these Games turned out almost as shambolic as the previous version. Like 1900, they suffered from bad organisation, poor crowds and controversy; and like 1900, they proved a mere sideshow to the World Fair. Consequently, Paris and St Louis came to be bracketed as the 'Farcical Olympics'.

Baron de Coubertin, who had championed the Chicago bid, did not attend, subsequently declaring acerbically: "I had a sort of presentiment that the Olympiad would match the mediocrity of the town."

St Louis came in for a fair bit of criticism which was to become something of a norm for future Olympic venues. "Its drinking water is a muddy brown – too thick to drink and too thin to plough," one newspaper editorialised. Athletics had to cope with the usual humid inferno of a Missouri summer.

None more so than the marathon runners who confronted a course laid out on poor dirt roads across seven low hills. Choking in the dust thrown up by the cars in front, the athletes suffered from cramps, vomiting and exhaustion in temperatures exceeding 90 degrees Fahrenheit. Without the provision of water, there was no relief and it was considered something of a miracle that no-one perished.

Against this background, the 1904 Olympic marathon assumed a prominent place in sporting infamy. Fred Lorz, a 24-year-old New York bricklayer and noted runner, was first out of the stadium and first to break the tape. In between, having suffered from terrible cramps which forced him to stop, he covered 11 of the 26 miles in his manager's car which broke down (perhaps from guilt) with six miles of the course remaining. Lorz managed to jog the rest of the way. He was about to have a laurel

wreath placed on his head by Alice, daughter of President Roosevelt, when his cheating was exposed. (President Roosevelt had
officially opened the games by symbolically pressing a golden but-
ton in the White House in Washington on receipt of a telegraph
signal from St Louis.)

Lorz had been spotted in a car. His openness – he was seen
smiling and waving to spectators and fellow runners when getting
in and out of the car – gave some backing to the view that Lorz
had not intended to cheat. Rather, his judgement had been affected
when receiving the cheers of the crowd on entering the stadium.
He continued to protest his innocence, arguing that he had run
the last few miles in order to avoid a chill and to fetch his clothes.

A claim, too, that his actions had been those of a practical
joker was later accepted with the rescinding of a lifetime ban in
time for him to enter and win the 1905 Boston Marathon. The
Olympic title went to English-born Thomas Hicks who in trying
to combat exhaustion with a dangerous concoction of strychnine
injections and brandy pretty nearly died in hospital. But he survived, never to run again. It is not known whether he also gave up
cocktails of rat poison and cognac.

Cheating and doping were almost acceptable when compared
to the so-called Anthropology Days, embarrassingly juxtaposed
with the Olympics, whereby with the overtly racist intention of
demonstrating the supremacy of Caucasians, 'uncivilised tribes' or
'savages', as they were called by the organisers, were encouraged
to try their hands at established sports. Without previous practice
these guinea pigs, some recruited from human zoo exhibits,
displayed understandable ineptitude. Even more shamefully, they
were persuaded with the promise of payment to take part in the
likes of greased-pole climbing, ethnic dancing and mud-slinging
for the titillation of white spectators.

Geronimo, the old Apache warrior, was at the age of 76
released from prison by the War Department to pose for photo-

graphs for which he received some remuneration. It is not known whether the native American regarded the money sufficient compensation for the humiliation.

America cleaned up on the medal front with a record haul of 242 gold, silver and bronze, not least because the hoped-for participation of athletes from around the world never happened. Different reports quote different figures but David Miller's *The Official History of the Olympic Games* and the IOC identifies a figure of 432 out of 687 official competitors representing the US.

It had been the desire of Messrs Lambert and McGrew when drawing up plans for the Olympic golf competition at Glen Echo to attract players from all over the world, though principally from the then golfing powerhouses of England and Scotland. To that end, Lambert visited the offices of *Golf Illustrated* in London in March 1904 in order to attract the support of British public opinion.

That was enough to prompt the prominent golf magazine of its day to reprint an article from the Chicago-based *Golfer's Magazine* illustrating the seriousness - some might say pomposity – in American thinking.

"This important contest," the American magazine declared, "...is in no sense of the word a World's Fair Championship, or a contest merely for pot hunters. It is the Olympic Championship of the World., and the winner will receive the Olympic gold medal, given by the Olympic Association... The Olympic Games is the only association worldwide in character, and which is capable of awarding a world championship's medal in amateur sport. It is this association which will rule supreme in the golf contest at the Glen Echo Country Club and although played under the rules of the USGA (United States Golf Association) that important body must give way to an even more important one than itself...

"We have champions of various countries, sectional champions and minor champions every year, but golf has never

31

had an Olympic champion (sic). It should mean something to even the best of British players to be able to hand down to posterity, as an heirloom, the Olympic Championship medal, the first and only one of its kind in the world... It is to be hoped that some of the very best of the British golfers will consider the honour of winning the Olympic Championship medal great enough glory to be a sufficient inducement for them to make the journey and compete. 'Tis the mere glory of winning a coveted title and of being the proud possessor of the distinguishing badge, not the intrinsic value of the prize itself, that makes the true amateur sportsman so keen to win it. The title 'Olympic Golf Champion' should certainly be as eagerly fought for as that of the Amateur Champion of Great Britain or the Amateur Champion of the United States.

"Even the glory of lasting to the semi-finals and securing one of the Olympic bronze medals should be tempting enough to attract the very best of our amateurs. Any amateur in the world is eligible to compete. The Maori chieftain, Kiropo Jarelia, who is amateur champion of New Zealand, or some crack young golfer who has learned the game on a public course, is just as eligible as the title holder in England or America. But what a battle royal it would be should the semi-finals be between two crack English players and two Americans, fighting it out between them for the final in the championship of the world."

Golf Illustrated, in turn, appeared to give Olympic golf its blessing. "It will be seen from the above," the magazine wrote in the same issue, "that our American cousins are throwing themselves into this matter with their accustomed energy and enterprise, and it is to be hoped that their efforts will meet with a due respect from golfers from all parts. Judging from the Exposition Bulletin and the photographs of the grounds and buildings which it contains, the St Louis Exhibition will be one of unparalleled size and beauty.

"The Olympic Golf Championship should be an additional attraction to any golfer who may be thinking of visiting the exhibition, and they should certainly take their clubs with them. In addition to the Olympic golf they are sure of an Olympian welcome and hospitality from our friends on the other side"

At least at that stage, six months out from the event, it was thought that some prominent British golfers of means might make the trip. Robert 'Bobby' Maxwell, a Scottish Etonian who won the Amateur Championship twice in 1903 and 1909, on both occasions at Muirfield where he was a member, and John Low, a captain of the Oxford and Cambridge Golfing Society who went on to chair the R&A Rules of Golf Committee, were mentioned in dispatches as likely entrants.

That proved sufficient for the *New York Evening Post* to report in April: "The foreign golfers have been in communication with the committee in charge of the tournament, and, it is said, a large representation will come from abroad. It is expected that some of the English players who comprise the Oxford and Cambridge Golfing Society team who toured America last year will return this summer to compete in the Olympic tournament."

By August, however, it had all gone quiet with *Golf Illustrated* almost despairingly asking: "Will none of our cracks who have the leisure and the wherewithal not make the voyage and bring back the World's Championship? It is surely an exploit worth attempting."

There was a major problem, however. No structure existed at the time for the selection of a British international team and individual golfers were naturally reluctant to become involved. They wanted to shoulder neither the responsibility nor the finance. The function of the R&A at that time extended no further than presiding over the Rules of the Game.

Not everyone shared the *Golf Illustrated* view of the Olympic event. *The Irish Golfer* magazine, for example, sounded a vitriolic trumpet against golf in the Olympics which was to be echoed in golfing corridors of power for most of the 20th century.

It wrote: "The Olympic Association may call the golf competition which it promotes the World Championship or the 'The Supremacy of the Utmost Surreal Horizon' or any other high-sounding title which rings sweetly in American ears; nevertheless, a grandiose title cannot, per se, give prestige to a meeting. It is only the recognition of the importance of the meeting, recognition in the form of the majority of the greatest golfers taking part, year after year, that can give prestige. A golf tournament, if it is to be seriously regarded as the World Championship, must be under the control of the old and famous golf clubs, and it must take place upon a course approved of by them as a proper test of the game.' Ouch.

It had been imagined that, like Paris, there would be a women's golf event in St Louis. But the IOC was still against the participation of women in the Olympics with Pierre de Coubertin a notorious opponent. He regarded the notion of women competing in the Games as "incorrect, unpractical, uninteresting and unaesthetic." A scandalous IOC statement declared: "We feel that the Olympic Games must be reserved for the solemn and periodic exaltation of male athleticism with internationalism as a base, loyalty as a means, art for its setting, and female applause as its reward."

In the aforementioned George McGrew – a member of the St Louis Games committee as well as the owner of Glen Echo – the IOC found a willing spokesman. "The admission of women to the Olympic Games would be too great a departure from the classic ideal," he said. "In olden times women were not even allowed to see the Games. To be sure the old notion about the presence of women at athletic contests has passed away, and this year in St Louis women will be among the most interested spectators. A golf tournament for women in the Olympic Games would be one of the most picturesque features of the whole contest if it were possible for them to be admitted, but as yet I see no chance for women being admitted to any of the Olympic contests, golf included."

So it was that on September 19, 2004, a field of 80 men – 77 Americans and three Canadians – embarked on the first of two qualifying rounds with the leading 32 on aggregate after the second round going through to the knock-out match play stages the following week. Not a single golfer from outside North America had made the journey. Indeed, precious few from the east coast of America had headed west. Known apathy of New Yorkers for any Western event had kicked in.

The whole occasion had a holiday feel to it, what with the inclusion of a long-driving competition, a novel putting contest at night under electric light, handicaps events, and competitions for non-qualifiers and match play losers. Only two were Olympic events, namely the 36-hole stroke play team event on September 17 and the individual match play during the week of 19 to 24 September from which would emerge the Olympic champion. Of the six 10-man teams entered, only two showed up, representing Western Golf Association and Trans-Mississippi Golf Association. A third USGA team was thrown together at the last minute. Western, headed by the recently crowned US Amateur champion, H Chandler Egan, won easily.

"The Western Golf Association team was composed entirely of young men of Chicago. These youngsters are a rather shifty lot of golfers," the *Globe* somewhat mysteriously – and perhaps a little bitterly – commented.

Egan, who in later life was to become a noted golf course architect, had already taken the long-hitting prize with drives of 234 and 202 yards, modest by today's standards. One hundred years of equipment development has added roughly 100 yards to the driving length of golfers.

With the late withdrawal of Walter J Travis, who that summer had become the first American to win the Amateur Championship at Royal St Georges, Egan arrived in St Louis as the firm favourite for Olympic gold. Although just turned 20, the Harvard University student was already viewed as a young giant. This was more to do with the impression given by his broad shoulders, slender waist and athletic physique than actual measurements of 5ft 11 and 180lbs.

Egan qualified for the match play stages easily enough with rounds of 88 and 78. But one report described him as "stale and over-golfed", having won the US Amateur only the previous week. Eleven of the 32 qualifiers were locals from St Louis; six of those progressed into the last 16 with Albert Lambert being defeated in the quarter final by the eventual champion.

While Egan strolled through the knock-out stages to the final with the minimum of inconvenience, there emerged from the other half of the draw, enjoying an even less troubled journey, a Canadian by the name of George Lyon, one of only three non-Americans in the competition.

Lyon was a fascinating character. A native born Canadian of Scottish and Irish descent – "I am a wee bit of Irish and a good bit of Scotch," he described himself – the insurance salesman did not take up golf until the age of 38, by which time he had established a reputation as one of Canada's finest cricketers. An innings of 238 not out in one afternoon for his club Rosedale was at the time the highest ever score made in Canada. Lyon represented his country on eight occasions, including four games against England and one against Australia.

This was a true all-rounder. At 18, he established a national record in pole vault, albeit with a height of a mere 10ft 6inches. Lyon was said to have excelled at hockey, rugby union and ten-pin bowling and to have been accomplished at football, tennis and curling. He was also well known as the captain of a local amateur baseball team.

It was while waiting in vain for the rain to stop at his cricket club in the autumn of 1895 that a friend and member of Rosedale Golf Club goaded Lyon into giving golf a go. He did so reluctantly but with some initial success in striking a few decent blows.

Writing for *Golf Illustrated* in 1906, he told the tale. "I was first induced to play the Royal and Ancient game by Mr Juno Dick, a member of the Rosedale Golf Club," Lyon wrote. "It happened this way. I was up at Rosedale cricket ground waiting for some of the players to come up for practice when Mr Dick came along with his golf clubs and said to me, "Come with me, Lyon, and have a try at golf.'

"I felt like saying to him 'Tipcat' [a child's game of the time] but of course wishing not to be rude I did so. Still, I had a bit of contempt for the game, though I had never played it. However, he prevailed upon me to go and try a drive from the first tee, which was nearby. Well, we went out to the tee and he teed a ball and gave me a driver and told me what to do. I remember I drove a fairly good ball, and then when I came up to it he gave me an iron and told me to play at the flag. I will not say any more about my short game as I fear I took too many strokes to be counted. Besides, I cared very little for what was called the short game.

"We went to the second tee and again I drove a fairly good ball, and this seemed to please me, so I kept going from one hole to the other until I had completed the full course of nine holes. I caught the (golf) fever there and then. I asked to be proposed as a member the next day."

Lyon already suffered from chronic hay fever, an occupational hindrance for a surprising number of golfers. He was no stylist. He possessed what one observer categorised as a "coal-heaver's swing" and was said "to lurch like a baby elephant." His unorthodox method brought ridicule from the purists.

By the Olympics, however, he had won three of his eight Canadian Amateur titles, the last in 1914 aged 56. Lyon was runner-up in the US Amateur in 1906 and a beaten semi-finalist in the Amateur Championship at Royal St Georges in 1908. He was also runner up in the Canadian Open in 1910 before going on to become Canada Seniors Golf champion 10 times between 1918 and 1930. In 1955 he was inducted into the Canadian Sports Hall of Fame and in 1971 he entered the Canadian Golf Hall of Fame.

His appointment as first chairman of The Canadian Golf Association's Rules Committee seemed appropriate to someone who, though affable and humorous, was renowned as a stickler for rules. There was a story told of an incident at the Toronto City Finals at Lambton Golf & Country Club when his opponent hooked his tee shot at the 18th into the billiard room. Lyon apparently made the unfortunate man play his next back onto the fairway from on top of the billiard table and through a window. The opponent was Lyon's elder son, Seymour, who lost both hole and match.

There is little question of the importance of Lyon in the development of Canadian golf. Karen Hewson, director of the Canadian Golf Hall of Fame and Museum, has likened Lyon to Francis Ouimet who won the US Open in 1913 and, inspiring a generation, became known as 'the father of amateur golf in America.' "He (Lyon) is certainly among the top half-dozen figures in the history of the game here. His impact was immense," Hewson said.

The Olympic final offered an obvious contrast between the 46-year-old who, with his greying temples and moustache, looked even older and the clean-shaven student 26 years his junior; between the Canadian in his flat cap and buttoned up dark jacket with breast pocket handkerchief and the American in short-sleeved shirt and light-coloured trousers.

The start of the 36-hole final was delayed because of a heavy downpour which left standing water on the greens. It continued to rain throughout a chilly morning first round. Lyon, blasting prodigious drives, won four of the first five holes and reached the turn three up. By lunch he had been pegged back to just a one-hole advantage.

The afternoon saw the sun come out, the heat rise and, surprisingly perhaps, the younger man wilt. Historian Jim Healey wrote: "In the second round Egan's game collapsed. The problem was his driving which was surprising since he had won the driving contest." (Lyon had arrived too late for that.) Lyon, who had never previously played competitively in the United States, went on to win comfortably by the margin of 3 and 2.

"The iron nerves of the older man, with his preponderating wisdom, born of longer experience, and the tremendous power pack of his drives, enabled him to carry off the honours in long play," the *Globe* reported.

The Post quoted both men in the aftermath. "I came to St Louis little expecting that I would gain the title of Olympic Golf Champion," Lyon said. "I attribute my success principally to my long drives. I outdrove Egan and it was mainly through this that I won."

Egan commented: "I am very sorry to have lost the match. I had nothing to gain and everything to lose. My opponent was the better player. Candidly speaking, I would have been surprised very much if I had won. I was stale from overplaying. After this year, I shall retire from the game and do not expect to play for many years to come. I graduate from Harvard this June and then enter the commercial world."

Bizarrely, Lyon celebrated victory by walking through the clubhouse dining room on his hands. But he had no illusions about his feat, waving aside claims to being champion of the world due to the absence of British golfers. "I am not foolish enough to think that I am the best player in the world," Lyon told the *Toronto Star*, "but I am satisfied that I am not the worst."

Lyon's gold medal was to disappear in the mists of time. A medal reissued by the IOC in 1997 today hangs on the wall at

Rosedale. His trophy is on display at the Canadian Golf Hall of Fame.

The absence of any British players – never mind some of the leading ones – clearly reduced coverage of the event on these islands to the bare minimum. *Golf Illustrated*, which had been favourably disposed towards the concept, managed just a single paragraph in its October 14 issue. It wrote: "The Olympics or World Championships at St Louis was rather a fizzle - that is to say, from the Olympic point of view. No English or Scottish golfers competed and the victor was Mr G S Lyon who has been champion of Canada. He beat Mr Chandler Egan, the new American champion in the final."

And that was that. Few, though, imagined that it would be another 112 years before golf made a third appearance in the Olympic Games. Officially, anyway.

4

SANDWICH GOLF IS TOAST

The only person to turn up for the 1908 London Olympic Games golf competition was the defending champion – George Lyon. In the absence of any opposition, the event was cancelled and Lyon was offered a second gold medal to add to the one hung over his neck in St Louis in 1904. Being a thoroughly decent chap, who would never countenance such a hollow 'victory', Lyon declined.

Thus ended yet another Olympic fiasco, one which it might be reasonable to suggest represented the moment when golf missed the opportunity to establish itself on the Olympic programme.

Unlike the so-called Farcical Games of 1900 and 1904, this particular piece of nonsense involved a protracted feud between those who did and did not want golf to have anything to do with the Olympic Games, set against some pretty crazy arrangements for the event.

It was not until two days prior to the scheduled start on June 1st that an official announcement of the cancellation of the championships was made. *The Times*, a leading voice in a vast media majority against golf being on the programme, carried the following item that morning: "It was officially announced on Saturday," it wrote, "that the Olympic golf competitions, fixed to take place today, tomorrow and on Wednesday, had been abandoned. The explanation of the British Olympic Association is that a number of British golfers sent in their names, but did not conform with the regulations in filling up the entry forms. These forms were, therefore, returned to the players with a request that the desired particulars be given; but, as they had not been received by the association on Saturday, there is nothing to do but abandon the fixture."

Actually, the entry forms had been deliberately filled in wrongly by golfers who were against the concept. By assuming this hostile stance, the prominent amateurs of the day were merely following a dictate of the Royal and Ancient Club of St Andrews. The R&A had made their opposition known months earlier, though only after an unseemly row with the BOA which had been played out in the newspapers and golf magazines.

It is necessary to return to 1906 to trace the origins of the disagreement. The Liberals are in government under the leadership of Henry Campbell-Bannerman; Edward VII is King; the British Empire covers one fifth of the world; James Braid wins the Open Championship at Muirfield with a score of 300.

Over in Greece, which is still fighting to stage the Olympics in perpetuity, what came to be known as the Interim Games are held in Athens. Despite – or perhaps because of – the event not being recognised officially by the International Olympic Committee, the Games are hugely successful with large crowds enthusiastically supporting the mainly high performance efforts of 826 competitors from 20 countries.

It was then that Rome, who had originally been awarded the 1908 Olympics, revealed it would be unable to host the Games. The reason given by Italy was that the country had been bankrupted by the massive volcanic eruption of Vesuvius which destroyed most of Naples. In fact, the decision to withdraw as hosts had been taken beforehand.

Britain, who had recently established a new National Olympic Committee, was invited to step into the breach. Enter William Henry Grenfell, later Lord Desborough of Taplow. Lord

Desborough, as he is always referred to, had been a runner, a rower and a swimmer, among many other things, good enough to run for Oxford and accomplished enough to take part in the Boat Race. He rowed across the English Channel in an eight and swam across the base of Niagara Falls. Twice. He climbed the Matterhorn by three separate routes and hunted big game in Africa.

Lord Desborough, who had been elected the first chairman of the NOC, was in Athens as the 50-year-old captain of the British Fencing Team. Leadership came naturally – and, it has to be said, frequently – to him. At various times in his life, he was President of the All England Lawn Tennis and Croquet Club, President also of the Amateur Fencing Association and, as if that were all not enough, President of the MCC. (He had, in fact, played at Lord's for Harrow.)

Within a few months, having lobbied for support among all his business and sporting contacts back home, Lord Desborough felt in a position to inform the IOC that Britain would be able to take over from Rome as the hosts of the fourth Olympic Games.

For the third occasion in a row the Olympics were linked to a World Fair. Instead of being an unwanted appendage, however, the Games became the centrepiece of the Franco-British Exhibition. The Exhibition put its money where its vocal support was by funding a spanking new main stadium at Shepherd's Bush, later to be called the White City. Somewhat oddly, it featured a cycle track around the outside of a running track – again provided by Charles Perry, the Stamford Bridge groundsman – and a swimming pool in the centre, all surrounded with seating for 68,000 spectators.

Come the big day, or rather the big weeks and months of the summer of 1908, the weather was miserable, a notable exception being the baking hot day on which – would you Adam and Eve it – the marathon was held. It rained, for example, throughout the tennis at Wimbledon. So what's new? The rowing was staged, perfectly understandably, at Henley while the sailing was held at the Isle of Wight and on the River Clyde, the only occasion in which Scotland has hosted an Olympic event.

It would be too much of an exaggeration to say the Games proved an unmitigated success: ticket prices were too high for the working class and, consequently, attendances were poor. Nationalism reared its sometimes ugly face at the opening ceremony while rampant prejudice by British judging officials created a rift between hosts and Americans which in sporting terms lasted for many years.

The marathon was twofold notable: with Queen Alexandra requesting that the race begin beneath the windows of the royal nursery in the grounds of Windsor Castle and with one circuit of the stadium track being added to a measured course of 26 miles the classic distance of 26 miles and 385 yards became established for time immemorial; and in the befuddled staggering round the track the wrong way of Italian Dorando Pietri, the Games had its 42.195km hero.

Crowds have a history of responding enthusiastically to a faltering marathon runner rendered pretty much senseless by the demands of the race. Pietri fell into that category. On the subject of falling, Pietri appears to have done quite a lot of it during a final lap which took 10 minutes to complete, once he had been pointed in the right direction. The little pastry cook from Carpi, near Modena, had been wrongly identified in the programme by being listed as P Dorando. The spectators may have been shouting unwittingly for Dorando but they were correct in recognising his distress.

He fell for what looked like the last time close to the line. What happened next was described in print by Sir Arthur Conan Doyle, who used the present tense for dramatic effect. "He (Pietri) staggers up, no trace of intelligence upon his set face, and again the red legs break into their strange automatic ramble. Will he fall again? No – he sways and balances: there he is through the tape and into friendly arms."

Great stuff from the creator of Sherlock Holmes, except that it did not happen like that. The dramatic description of his fiction had intruded into his reportage. Pietri was picked up and carried across the line by two men who should have known better, the chief supervisor of the race and the medical officer. A protest was lodged successfully on behalf of the next person through the winning line, Johnny Hayes of the USA, and the Italian was stripped of his 'victory'.

The following day the Queen presented Pietri with a special gold cup and a handwritten message (which again used his Christian name as his surname) stating: "For P Dorando, In Remembrance of the Marathon Race, From Windsor to the Stadium, From Queen Alexandra."

In subsequent interviews to his national press, which the Italian National Olympic Committee provided for David Miller in his book, *The Official History of the Olympic Games and the IOC*, Dorando explained why he became so confused and disorientated after taking the lead inside the final few miles. "Now I was first, I could have slowed down but I was seized by a fury to go even faster," he declared. "With the road ahead clear, I could not put a brake on myself. The runners passed between lines of spectators on both sides. In my frenzy I could not see them, but I heard them. Suddenly, my heart gave a jump. I saw a grey mass in front that seemed a bastion with the bridge beflagged. It was the stadium. And after that, I remember little."

The Games belonged to the host nation. Britain won 145 medals to the 47 of the United States. America prevailed, as ever, in track and field while Britain scooped up all the gold medals in boxing, rowing, sailing and tennis. These had been the first games in which entries were by nations rather than individuals. This lay in the future.

In July 1906 a letter, signed by Lord Desborough, was sent

to the Royal and Ancient Club at St Andrews, as the controlling body of golf, and to other governing bodies of sport, stating that the BOA had been asked to hold the Olympic Games in England in 1908. The letter gave reasons why the invitation should be accepted and asked the R&A, along with the other bodies, to lay the matter before its committee and to nominate a representative to serve on the council of the BOA for the organising of the Games.

To this day the R&A claim never to have received the letter. Peter Dawson, who retired as chief executive in 2015, says that investigations have been conducted. "The R&A sometimes gets the blame (for golf not being in the 1908 Olympics) but I rush to our defence saying that we can find no record of that letter. There is not only no record of receiving it but there is no reference made about it in all the minutes of the meetings."

Could it have been lost in the post? Of course it could have been, judging by the record of the Post Office. Might it have been thrown in the bin by an R&A administrator who regarded golf in the London Olympics as only marginally better than a woman in the clubhouse? Perhaps. We will never know. What we know for certain is that the BOA did not write a second time, an action which might have revealed the disappearance of the original communication. And what we can infer from that is that the BOA did not really want a response from golf's ruling body because it was perfectly aware of what it would be.

In the absence of R&A involvement, the BOA persuaded H Ryder Richardson, the secretary of Royal St Georges at Sandwich in Kent and Honorary Secretary of the Amateur Championship, to take charge of the proposed Olympic golf event. Richardson was one of those secretarial martinets who ruled their domain with iron fists, an administrator who would prompt a shiver of apprehension among club members and visiting players.

His task was never going to be easy given the battalions lined up in opposition. Come Christmas 1907, the editor of *Golf*

Illustrated, Gordon G Smith, weighed in with a pre-emptive strike. "An Olympic golf contest is being dimly foreshadowed for the coming season," he wrote. "It does not appeal to us as attractive or desirable from any point of view. There was an Olympic Golf Championship held at St Louis a year or two ago…which its promoters declared was to settle the Golf Championship of the World. Magnificent prizes were offered, the event was advertised, and golfers were invited from all quarters of the Globe. We are not aware that a single British or any golfer crossed the Ocean to contest the possession of the chief trophy, or the right to the proud title of Olympic Golf Champion, both of which were won by Mr G S Lyon, from Canada.

"Doubts were felt, and freely expressed at the time, as to the right of the promoters of the St Louis Exhibition to institute a championship of such pretensions, but none were either felt or expressed as to the value of the title after the event. It is to be hoped that the Shepherd's Bush authorities (BOA) will show a truer sense of proportion in the designation they may adopt for their proposed golf exhibition or tournament.

"In any case, golfers will want to know a great deal more about the origin and purport of the project before they can be expected to enthuse over it; but its promoters may rest assured of two things – that if it is advertised as a world championship, or by any such pretentious designation, or if it is in the least degree subsidised or engineered by trading interests, our amateurs will have nothing to do with it."

Nevertheless, Richardson pressed on. The strength of Scotland and England, and to a lesser extent Ireland and Wales, in world golf persuaded officialdom that each should be represented in the Olympic team event. To this end, Richardson proposed that with Great Britain providing four teams all other countries should be permitted to field four teams.

Gaskets were blown, especially in Scotland. John L Low,

chairman of the championship committee of the Royal and Ancient and one of amateur golf's pre-eminent world figures, wrote to *The Scotsman* newspaper characterising the absurdity of conditions by which Belgium (for example) would be allowed to send four teams to the Olympics and Scotland only one. Low's letter was backed up by the opinions of nine of the leading amateurs in the country, most notably John Ball and Robert Maxwell.

That was when Rev R S de Courcy Laffan, the honorary secretary of the BOA, revealed that the R&A had failed to reply to Lord Desborough's letter in the summer of 1906. Back came Low, who had become the de facto leader of the 'no' campaign, with a letter to *Golf Illustrated* who also received a statement from St Andrews on high.

"Sir, I am requested by the Green committee of the Royal & Ancient, who have had their attention drawn by letters in the public press to the proposed Olympic competition, to state that they have received no circular on the subject from the Olympic Council referred to in the correspondence. Had any such communication been received the Green Committee would have placed the matter before the general meeting of the club in September 1906. I am, Sir, etc, CS Grace, Hon Sec Green Committee, St Andrews 20th Jan 1908."

Golf Illustrated gave their opinion: 'We can see nothing in this Olympic golf meeting which is likely to add to the honour and glory of the game, and we see many possibilities of a cheapening and degradation of the game in irresponsible and unnecessary championships of this nature. On the evil of the multiplication of championships we have always spoken in terms of strong condemnation. If the Olympic Championships are to vie with the present Open and Amateur Championships, no loyal supporter of golf will have anything to do with them. If this is not their aim, then they have no meaning and are but one more unnecessary and harmful addition to the many bastard championships which already exist."

Newspaper opinion was almost entirely negative. *The Morning Post* wrote that there was "something quite inappropriate about the inclusion of golf in the Olympic programme"; the *Edinburgh Evening Dispatch* took the view that "international golf of this kind suddenly organised by wholly irresponsible authorities is apt to prove a fiasco, and in consequence do harm instead of good to the game. Golf is altogether foreign to the games associated with the famous Greek gathering"; the *Daily Chronicle*, seeing fault on both sides, commented that there was "much that is undesirable about the atmosphere of golf, and if contests that are called international are going to be promoted without the sanction of the authorities we all recognise (however much those authorities may at times have laid themselves open to the charge of being old fashioned and stagnant) we are going to arrive at a most regrettable state of affairs."

By the beginning of 1908 the battle lines and the arguments were clearly drawn. HH Hilton, writing in the Western Morning News of January 24, articulated the objections as fourfold: that no golf was played at the ancient games; that the existing Amateur and Open championships are to all intents the championships of the world, open to the world; that the championship links of Great Britain are the finest in the world, and in other countries it is at present not possible to get links of the Briritsh standard of merit; that the Royal and Ancient and all right-minded golfers are opposed to exploiting golf for any purpose.

De Courcy Laffan responded with a press release which attempted to deal with the objections on a point by point basis.

■ That is perfectly true, It is also true that the stadium at Olympia was not lighted by electricity. The one fact is as germane as the other to the question how modern Olympic Games should be conducted. The modern Olympic Games are not an archaeological revival. We do not include in our programme chariot races, horse races or pankration [a combination of boxing and wrestling]. We do include rowing, swimming, cycling, football, fencing and many other sports which found no place in the ancient games. If the important associations which govern these sports are undertaking the management of them in the Olympic Games of London it is a little difficult to see why it should be sacrilege to wish to include golf.

■ It is not easy to see the point of this remark. We have never called our golf competitions 'championships' or suggested that they should be considered as deciding who is the golf champion of the world. The Olympic Games were designed, as far as possible, to include all the sports of the modern world which have attained an international position. Mr Hilton will hardly deny that this is the case with golf.

■ This seems a curious reason for wishing to forbid Olympic golf on the said finest links in the world.

■ If by 'exploiting' Mr Hilton means 'deriving pecuniary profit' it is difficult to see how this can be true of a competition for which there are no entrance fees and no gate money. If he means that the BOC expects to derive some material advantage other than pecuniary from these competitions, the insinuation is one which, not being an admirer of the language which Mr Hilton quotes with so much delight, I prefer not to characterise. Your readers will judge for themselves of the value of a case which needs such insinuations to support it.

Golf Illustrated printed a range of press opinion including the following from the *Birmingham Post*, the *Evening Standard* and the *Manchester Guardian*.

Birmingham Post – (The Olympic contests) should provide an occasion for some interesting golf, unless the anathemas now rolling from the R&A Clubhouse frighten away most of the British leading players. Such, however, may be the result of Mr Low's action in piling so exceptionally heavy a mountain on the top of so ridiculously small a mouse.

Evening Standard – Does not Mr Low, for whose opinions about the game everyone has, of course, the greatest respect, protest too much? There are those whose desire for competitions is never satisfied: their tastes may be abnormal, but are not criminal, and there seems no very clear reason why they should not indulge them. The very distinguished body of gentlemen who manage the Olympic Games have decided, not very wisely, as most people think, to include golf in their programme. Surely they might be allowed to do so in peace.

Manchester Guardian – One may wonder that the BOA did not take the somewhat obvious course of writing again to the Royal and Ancient, to know if their first letter was to receive any consideration. It would at least have revealed the loss of the first letter. Possibly the association thought it was not worthwhile throwing good stamps after bad ones. As Mr Low now points out 'it seems hardly possible that the Olympic Council could have thought that these proposed contests could have been considered by the R&A and that the Club could have taken no notice of such extraordinary proposals'.

Golf Illustrated even published a satirical poem on the row under its regular feature entitled 'The Caddie's Advice.'

> Cried a golfer, called – (whisper it 'low'!),
> "Your 'championship' meeting's de trop;
> May your lists of Olympia
> Grow skimpier and skimpier,
> Till they fizzle in flat fiasco!"

Shrieked Laffan, "O, lor! the 'low' language
Of St Andrews' belated harangue, which
Will frighten away,
So the critics all say,
Folks who else would have mustered at Sangwidge."

Cried the Caddie, "Stop using as missiles,
These fervid, but futile, epistles!
Let Laffan meet Low,
And the Victor Ludo—
Rum be crowned with a garland of thistles!"

Golf Illustrated further opined: "The severe criticisms of Mr Low and Mr Hilton, among others, on the Olympic project, have shown in the highest circles the idea is not welcomed. On the other hand, the British Olympic Association's golf representatives, by deprecating all idea of a championship and by defining their meeting as being attended to afford merely an international encounter at golf on the same lines as other international sports in the Olympic Games have to some extent cut the ground from under the feet of the opposers.

"There are enough championships and to spare as it is, and no element would be introduced into an Olympic Championship which is not already present in our existing championships. If the St Andrews manifesto has thwarted such a scheme in their minds, then they are entitled to our sympathy to the extent of having been metaphorically knocked down for an affront of which they were innocent.

"But even if the Olympic Association had no intention of setting up a fresh championship, and were inspired merely by the apparently laudable desire of making their meeting fully representative of modern sport as possible, we fear that we cannot see eye to eye with them in this matter. There does not seem to us to be enough connection between a golf tournament played at Sandwich and an Olympic festival held in London to make the thing either interesting or appropriate. It would only be a degree less absurd to have an Olympic Skating Championship held in the Fens in December and connect it with an Olympic festival held in London in June."

And so the debate raged through winter into spring and beyond. But it was probably the logistical nightmare dreamed up by the organisers rather than the principle which in the end did for plans to include golf in the London Olympics. Somehow, it was imagined that the British golfers would be prepared to endure playing 36 holes of stroke play on consecutive days at Royal St George's, Royal Cinque Ports and Prince's after having been required to qualify for the British teams at the prestigious St George's Vase competition a couple of weeks earlier followed by the Amateur Championship. As one commentator remarked, this represented more of an ordeal than "an Australian test match."

Criticism proved caustic. "Despairing, perhaps, of getting an 'Olympic' array of golfers for their projected competitions," *Golf Illustrated* wrote, "the Olympic Golf Committee have apparently made the best of a bad job by setting competitors an 'Olympian' task in the way of endurance."

The golf correspondent of the *Daily Mail* waved his quill in similar tones. "Thirty six holes," he wrote, "with a card and a pencil on each of three consecutive days is enough to make the boldest heart quake, at least momentarily. Certainly the winner will well deserve his laurel wreath, and it is only to be hoped that he will survive to wear it."

Ultimately, with only the defending champion present and willing to play, the Olympic golf event had to be cancelled.

You would think that would have been the end of thoughts of including golf in the Olympics at that time. Not a bit of it. Although no tournament was organised at the 1912 Games in

Stockholm, there being few courses in that country at that time, it was intended for golf to be part of the 1916 Games in Berlin, which of course was cancelled due to the Great War.

The plan was to build a new 18 hole course at Wannsee in Berlin, where years later Percy Alliss, father of Peter, Ryder Cup golfer and BBC Television commentator extraordinaire, became the professional. The land for the ambitious development was acquired from the Prussian Government in no small measure due to the personal intervention of Emperor Wilhelm II, son of Queen Victoria, and the golf-mad Crown Prince Henry.

A dispatch to the *New York Times*, dateline Berlin May 24, 1913, is delightful both for its headline and as a reminder of a time when a famous invention changed the nature of communication.

'CROWN PRINCE LIKES GOLF' the headline ran, followed by the stand-first 'Future Kaiser plays with English officers on Berlin Links' and the byline 'By Marconi Transatlantic Wireless Telegraph to the New York Times.'

The short piece read: "The Americans and English, who are moving spirits in the Berlin Golf Club, received the honour of a visit from the Crown Prince on their course in the West End on Wednesday afternoon. The Crown Prince, who was inoculated with the golf germ during his trip to India three years ago, has been a lover of the Royal and Ancient game ever since.

"He played 18 holes on Wednesday with Captain Watson, the naval attache, and Major Russell, the military attache at the British Embassy."

The previous week *The New York Times* reported that The Kaiser and Prince Henry of Prussia had actively supported plans to build a new course for Berlin Golf Club near Potsdam to replace its inadequate nine hole Rynold course in a suburb of the West End.

"Three quarters of the area is state property and is secured by a lease from the government authorities..." the article reported.

"...Prince Henry is an ardent and clever golfer. The new links, which will not be ready for play for 18 months, are destined to become internationally famous as the scene of golf contests of the Olympic games in the summer of 1916.

"They will be laid out in the finest possible style and no expenses will be spared to make them the peer of the best course in the world. The club's plans include the erection of a splendid country clubhouse on American and English models, while the propinquity of the new links to Potsdam will, it is believed, induce the young military set to take up golf with more interest than hitherto."

Christoph Meister, one of the foremost golf historians in Germany, takes up the story. "The trees were cut down and the fairways were seeded in 1913. Scottish architect Cuthbert Butchart was to have designed the new course at Wannsee. But the Great War intervened and it was a number of years after the end of hostilities before the project was restarted and finished."

Cuthbert Butchart was an interesting character. Born in Carnoustie in 1876, the son of a golf club manufacturer, he caddied at the nearby Barry course as a 14-year-old. Butchart went on to become a professional attached at various times to a host of golf clubs including Royal Mid Surrey, Pollock (Glasgow), Royal County Down and West Byfleet before moving to Germany. By then he had established himself not only as a player – he won the German Professional Championship in 1913 – but as one of the earliest professional golf instructors (an early day Butch Harmon, if you like), a golf club manufacturer and a golf course architect. His designs included Bangor, Hunstanton and Bad Kissingen in Bavaria.

Butchart was interned in Ruhleben prisoner of war camp where he was put in charge of sanitation and elected director of the prisoners' own police force. Ever the designer and creative spirit he taught himself while in the camp how to make jewellry

55

out of scrap metal. In 1921, aged 44, Butchart emigrated to New York to be processed, like so many immigrants, at Ellis Island. He died in America in 1955.

Still, golf's attempts to be an Olympic sport lingered. Almost stubbornly, when plans were being made to reignite the Olympic flame after World War I in Antwerp in 1920, golf appeared as little more than a dying ember on the preliminary schedule. It was even listed in the original programme.

But *The New York Times* was reporting that plans for both tennis and golf were in "uncertain condition". For golf, the newspaper stated, "the uncertainty is more pronounced and, accordingly, the Belgian Olympic Committee has failed to provide any dates for the links games, preferring to await definite information from the various countries which have planned representations."

Another *NYT* article did, however, mention the possibility of a men's and women's event taking place on July 12-15 at the Royal Antwerp Golf Club, to this day one of the finest wooded heathland courses on the continent. There was an accompanying health warning which noted: "NB, if the committee judges that the number of entries is insufficient, the competition will be cancelled."

That was precisely what happened.

5

THE GOLF FÜHRER

To Adolf Hitler, the Olympic Games was "an invention of Jews and freemasons." This was not meant as praise.

Adolf Hitler did not play golf and he did not drink alcohol. That in itself would have been enough to condemn him in the eyes of many. Yet, the same Adolf Hitler, no sports fan he, was to position himself as an omnipresent centrepiece of a 1936 Berlin Olympics which, had his agents been successful in their efforts, would have included golf, 32 years after its previous participation and a full eight decades before eventually being welcomed back into the fold.

How did this come about?

Hitler's conversion just a few months after stating that a National Socialist Germany could not host the Olympics was entirely down to Josef Goebbels who, though himself equally not enamoured by sport, recognised the value of the Games as a showpiece for the Third Reich. As the new Minister of Popular Enlightenment and Propaganda, with the accent very much on the latter, Goebbels persuaded his Führer to display enough enthusiasm for the project to satisfy the International Olympic Committee who had awarded Berlin the Games on May 13th, 1931. The IOC, for its part, seemed only too willing to turn a pair of blind eyes and a couple of deaf ears to events in Germany that could – indeed should – have led to Berlin losing the Games.

By the time the Games came around, Jews were "not permit-

baths for fear that they would infect the water,"
om equestrian clubs in case the German horses
Jewish riders", according to Guy Walters in his
Berlin Games. And in direct contravention of the
.ter which was supposed to assemble "the amateurs
of all na.. s on an equal footing", the new German government
passed a law on April 26 which banned Jews from membership
of sports organisations. Over a period of three months, Jews
were excluded from tennis competitions and gymnastic clubs. The
German Skiing Union, the German Boxing Federation and the
German Rowing Association – now all run by Nazi Party stooges
– all banned Jews.

The Spirit of Sport in the Third Reich, an oxymoron if ever there
was one, written by Bruno Malitz, a Nazi spokesman, stated gro-
tesquely: "There is no room in the German land for Jewish leadership in sport, nor for pacifists and those betrayers of the people,
the pan-Europeans, or others infected by Jews. They are worse
than cholera, tuberculosis, syphilis, worse than pillaging hordes of
Kalmucks, worse than fire, starvation, flood, drought, poison gas."

In August 1935, the Reich Sport Commissar announced that
sports clubs should set aside the month of October for teaching
anti-Semitism; in September the Nuremburg Laws were passed
depriving Jews of citizenship; shops refused to serve Jews and
citizens were forbidden from buying from stores owned by Jews.

Jewish sportsmen and sportswomen were effectively neutered.
Jews were denied facilities where they could train. Nor were they
allowed to represent their country, the ultimate sanction for any
ambitious sportsman or sportswoman. The fact that Germany
picked a few token Jews fooled no one, including the bend-over-
backwards IOC and the many, it has to be said, countries who
decided to send teams to Berlin – a total of 47, including Great
Britain, where there was not much of a campaign for a boycott,
and the United States, where the debate had been furious.

Ten thousand protesters gathered at Madison Square Garden to protest against America taking part in the 1936 Olympics. The American Athletic Union received more than 100,000 individual protests. Their annual convention in late 1935, a three-day jamboree of internecine warfare held at the Commodore Hotel in New York City, ended with a narrow majority in favour of attending the Games in Berlin.

In contrast, a general mood of appeasement prevailed in Britain, making it difficult to build up any real opposition to Olympic participation. The National Workers Sports Association led the way. Sir Walter Citrine, General Secretary of the Trades Union Council and head of International Federation of free Trade Unions backed a 32-page booklet entitled *Under the Heel of Hitler*, outlining the dictatorship over sport in Nazi Germany. Among others who came out publicly against the Games was *Isis*, the Oxford University magazine.

But Harold Abrahams, a Jew who himself experienced anti semitism on the way to winning the 100 metres gold medal at the Paris Olympics of 1924 (a story immortalised in the film *Chariots of Fire*), spoke out in favour of participation at a committee meeting of the British Olympic Association. And that was pretty much that.

Basically, his argument was that it was up to the IOC to withdraw from the Games not the British team. Abrahams wanted to participate precisely because things were bad in Germany whereas Avery Brundage, for example, a future IOC President and at that time President of the American Olympic Committee, was in favour because because he believed things in German were supposedly not as dreadful as they seemed. He carried the day in the States but it was a close call. America became the Pied Piper and the rest followed with the exception of Ireland, the only country to boycott the Berlin Games. It did so, however, for an entirely different reason – as a protest against the International Amateur

Athletic Federation suspending the National Athletic and Cycling Association (of Ireland) the previous year. Let us not go there...

Somewhat bizarrely, German golf wanted to get in on the act. As Georges Jeanneau wrote in his book *Golf and the Olympic Games*: "It is hard to explain the origin of such an event. Germany had no golfing tradition, nor champions, and only some 50 golf courses."

But Germany had plans for golf. As a headline in the *Chicago Tribune* declared: 'Golf, by Nazi decree, is to be a national sport of Germany.' The story stated that (under) "orders from Berlin, Karl Henkell, chief of the German Golf Club Union, and Gustav Schaeefer, leader of the Gymnastic and Sport Association, announced plans to popularise the Royal & Ancient game and bring it within the price reach of the lowest German."

The army, navy, Hitler's storm troops and members of the youth movement were expected to "lead a new horde of players across the German fairways." There were to be new and better courses; the price of equipment was to be lowered; and memberships of golf clubs would be limited to two Reichsmarks a year for adults and 1 mark for juniors under 18. Golfers would be ordered to speak German and use their own words for the likes of fairways, caddie and driver. The international language of golf has always been English.

The governing Nazi Party installed a new hierarchy in which the pyramid of power was changed from top to bottom. This was as true for sport (and golf) as it was for all other facets of life. The grandly named Herr Hans von Tschammer und Osten became Reichsportsfuhrer, the sports minister. He, in turn, appointed Dr Karl Henkell as President of the Deutsche Golfverband (the German Golf Association).

Henkell, the 'Golf Führer', as the legendary commentator Henry Longhurst christened him, placed sympathetic officials in charge of Germany's 48 golf clubs. He was anything but your average golf administrator. He became principle shareholder of the mighty Henkell wineries company, still going strong today, on the death of his nephew in 1940. Henkell's sister, the Lady Macbeth-like Annelies, had married Joachim von Ribbentrop in 1920, giving Hitler's notorious Foreign Minister the wealth to back up his social-climbing ambitions.

It was Henkell who, with war fast approaching, stamped a document helping British golfing legend Henry Cotton to get out of Germany quickly after winning the German Open. Armed with a Henkell-authorised pass but without his winner's cheque, Cotton drove his Rolls Royce at breakneck speed to Calais only to find long queues of cars waiting to cross the Channel. Nora Zahn, the German Golf Association secretary, ensured that Cotton received his 500 Reichsmark first prize and the trophy when the war was over.

Henkell was given the task of getting golf into the Olympics. Hitler may have disliked elitism and the games elitists played but he recognised the prestige carried by golf in Germany and understood its potential in promoting the new Germany. There was a 'British' atmosphere around golf that appealed. An approach was made to the IOC to add golf to the schedule. But it was too late, much too late. Making golf part of the Games was simply not possible as the participating sports had already been agreed upon at a much earlier date.

If not within the official Games, Henkell thought, then why not as a prestigious addendum? He busied himself arranging an international tournament that would be close enough in time if not place to be regarded as part of the Olympiad. Henkell came up with Der Grosse Preis der Nationen (The Grand Prize of Nations) which was designed to allow golf to wrap itself in the Olympic flag, at least metaphorically speaking.

"There is no question that this was the most important golf event to have been held in Germany at that time," the German golf historian Christoph Meister said.

Baden-Baden, an elegant spa resort situated in the pine-clad foothills of the Black Forest, was chosen as the location for a gathering which the aforementioned Tschammer und Osten deemed would also include two other non-Olympic sports, tennis and horse racing. Wealthy Romans had holidayed there 2,000 years earlier. But Baden-Baden did not begin to flourish until the 19th century when it became a magnet for the smart set of Europe. American diplomats took their annual vacation there while British nobility chose it as a place to recover from the London season or cure rheumatic limbs in the hot thermal springs. They would flirt with each other and with the whims of the roulette wheel.

The three Russian 'Ys', so to speak, Tolstoy, Dostoevsky and Tschaikovsky, were devotees, as was Queen Victoria. Indeed, Fyodor Dostoevsky wrote his novelette *The Gambler* after losing all his money in the Baden-Baden casino in 1863.

Henkell hoped that through his global network of business associates and influential people, he might persuade golfers from around the world to compete for the Grand Prize. To that end – and more generally to promote German golf – Henkell led a party of up to 20 distinguished members of German golf clubs on an American tour in February and March of 1936.

Henkell had scarcely rediscovered his land legs after the boat trip from Hamburg to New York before he found himself playing – and being photographed – with a smiling club co-founder Bobby Jones in the shadow of the iconic loblolly pines at Augusta National. A return four ball involving Jones and Henkell took place in Berlin later that year in the run up to the Olympics where the American golfing legend took his seat as an honoured guest.

Invitations for the golf at Baden-Baden were sent to 36 countries. In the event, only six turned up. Embarrassingly for the hosts, 28 nations declined with Switzerland and Sweden, having initially accepted, withdrawing just two days before the start. There is no question that the changing nature of the country under Nazi rule and the horror stories coming out of Germany played a significant part in the boycott. Specifically, golfers everywhere did not take kindly to the government edict that German golf clubs scratch Jewish members from the list of members.

England was one of the half dozen to accept, along with France, Italy, Czechoslovakia, Hungary and The Netherlands, though it is fair to say there were doubters and debates in all of those countries.

Golf Illustrated, a prominent voice at the time, was unhappy with the decision and said so unequivocally in an editorial on August 8, 1936. "The British golfing public will regret England's participation in the forthcoming International Golf Tournament at Baden-Baden," it wrote, "which is a sort of backwash of the Olympic Games at present being held in Germany. It will regret still more the details of that participation.

"The EGU (English Golf Union), having accepted a seat on the committee, proceeded to invite Messrs Francis Francis and A L Bentley to represent England on the understanding that they should pay their own expenses. We submit that if the EGU considered this tournament worthy of its official notice they should have taken the necessary steps to select the best pair possible to represent England, and in order to do that they should have undertaken to bear all expenses connected with the adventure. If they were unable to do that, as they obviously were in the light of the Walker Cup match, they should have left the matter severely alone.

"It is our humble opinion that these international tournaments are opposed to the true spirit of sport and violate the conscience of the British public. We look upon sport as a relaxation, and as a means of promoting a friendly camaraderie distinct of colour, creed and nationality. That is just what the Olympic Games and all its attachment fail to do, and everyone with the interests of golf at heart should strive might and main to keep it away from the atmosphere of intense nationalism existing at all these Games. From every point of view the EGU's decision in this matter must be considered a most unfortunate one."

It would appear from those remarks that *Golf Illustrated* was against international competition per se rather than the fact that this was a German government-sponsored event. Further, the magazine seemed hostile to the Olympic movement as a whole rather than the specific Berlin Games. At any rate, it kept up the attack the following week under a heading 'Keep Golf Away from This.'

The Editorial read: "In *Golf Illustrated* of last week we deplored the English Golf Union's decision to be represented in the International Golf Tournament which is being run in Baden-Baden in connection with the Olympic Games. In the light of the fracas between the Peruvian and Austrian football teams we deplore the EGU's decision still more.

"As reported, the match between Peru and Austria produced thoroughly disorderly behaviour, including revolver shots and a free fight among the players. The International Football Federation, having ordered the match to be replayed, the Peru team withdrew from the Games, while a disreputable attack was made on the German consulate in Lima.

"It…seems an inevitable counterpart of all these Olympic gatherings. Such incidents must nauseate all true sportsmen, and where golfers are concerned make them all the more determined to keep golf away from such a poisonous atmosphere. The English Golf Union have made many mistakes: they have never made a bigger one than this."

(The *Golf Illustrated* reference to Olympic football is worth a brief explanation for those who are either unaware of the incident or have forgotten the details. Briefly, Austria, managed by Englishman Jimmy Hogan, played Peru in the quarter finals. Austria, afforded Aryan support in the absence of the host nation, led 2-0 at half time only for the Peru to draw level. The Peruvians had three goals disallowed in the first half of extra time by the Italian referee before scoring twice to lead 4-2.

With only minutes remaining a pitch invasion led to an Austrian player suffering a leg injury. The match was abandoned. The Peruvians declared it a Nazi conspiracy, staged to sabotage a victory for a South American side containing five black players. The Austrians claimed the invading fans were excited Peruvians, a version backed up by reports in British newspapers.

A replay was ordered. The whole Peruvian Olympic team, insisting they would not get a fair deal, packed up and went home. Colombia did likewise out of solidarity. Anti-German protests followed in Peru with dockers refusing to load goods onto German ships. In the absence of Peru, Austria advanced to the semi-final where they defeat Poland. Italy won the final 2-1.)

Hitler would have been annoyed at the high number of refusals for the Baden-Baden tournament. He had, after all, personally gifted the trophy which would be presented to the champions. The unique 36 centimetre silver-gilt salver was inlaid with eight six centimetre amber circular panels. The stamp 'L' identified it as the creation of famous German goldsmith Emile Lettre who at one time had been appointed to the Berlin Court and operated from those celebrated workshops at Unter-den-Linden. The distinctive yoke-like amber stone was classically German, found on the southern shores of the Baltic.

The engraving in the centre left no doubt about the importance of the event and the identity of the donor. Over five lines, one above the other, it read: GOLFPREIS der NATIONEN, GEGEBEN VOM, FUHRER und REICHSKANZLER, BADEN-BADEN, 1936.

In English, 'Golf Prize of Nations, given by, Leader and Reich Chancellor, Baden-Baden, 1936.'

Given the provenance of the trophy, there was little doubt that the organisers would press on with plans. Could it be that, given the 'correct' result, Herr Hitler would journey to Baden-Baden to hand over his own trophy? That was a question for the future.

The event was to be even grander than the silverware suggested. A 'Grosser' was added along the way so that when the rules and regulations were distributed the tournament had become Grosser Golfpreis der Nationen or Grand Prize of Nations. This was perhaps to tie in with the racing at Iffezheim Racecourse which dated back to 1858 when the big race on opening day was the Grosser Preis von Baden.

The race exists today, a Group 1 for flat horses over a mile and a half on the first September weekend of the year. The historic race, which was part of the post-Olympic sporting carnival in Baden-Baden has been won by legendary jockeys such as Frankie Dettori, Keiron Fallon, Willie Carson, Pat Eddery, Walter Swinburn and American Steve Cauthen. Further kudos came its way in 2012 when it was added to the Breeders Cup Challenge Series with the winner gaining an automatic invitation to the Breeders Cup Turf.

Arrangements for the Grand Prize of Nations were put in place by Nora Zahn, whose secretaryship of the German Golf Union spanned a period of 40 years until 1968 and was the person more responsible than any other for the growth of golf in Germany. Well known to all the leading British professionals and amateurs, she gained the reputation of having no equal in terms of organising tournaments, from the German Open down to the most humble amateur event.

Further evidence of how much this international competition was regarded as Olympic in everything but IOC recognition were the Conditions of Play. Entries could be made only by the countries, not individuals, and the players themselves were required to comply with national status as defined by the Olympic Committee.

A letter from the President of Baden-Baden Golf Club to the Mayor of Baden-Baden, signed off with a Heil Hitler greeting, requested 5,400 Reichsmarks from city funds to help pay for an occasion he described as "the most important tournament ever held in Germany."

Such an esteemed event demanded glittering prizes, bearing in mind the players were amateur and subject to the strict status rules imposed by the R&A. First prize, of course, was the unique plate from the workshop of Professor Lettre that became known as The Hitler Trophy. Second prize was a rather magnificent Meissen vase donated by the Reich Sports Minister while the third placed team would receive a Karl Lang-Hanau silver box courtesy of the Federal Governer of Baden-Baden.

Back in Britain the English Golf Union, denied Walker Cup players because of the clash of events, set about selecting a team.

6

FLOUR POWER

It is not known whether the wonderfully named and doubly sainted Francis Francis considered selection for the two-man England team for the post-Olympic international tournament at Baden-Baden so much of a hot potato that he dropped it, and himself.

The reason is lost in the mists of the links. His late withdrawal might have been due to illness since only ill health or a sudden emergency were accepted in the conditions of play as valid reasons. The same Francis had pulled out of the 1928 Olympic Games due to ill health, having being picked to represent Great Britain in three sports, including athletics and fencing. In any event, the multi-millionaire informed the English Golf Union that he would be unable to play just seven days prior to the scheduled start.

His son, Craig, the former owner of Caribbean Shipping who splits his time between Switzerland and the Bahamas and is well known to his fellow members at Sunningdale, was aware of the Olympic connection, but had no idea about his father's selection for the Baden-Baden tournament until contacted by the author.

Francis Francis would have been a fascinating participant with a back story, as they say, as juicy as it comes. Francis was born in London in 1906, the son of Francis Francis and Frances Evelyn Bostwick. He was a 15-year-old schoolboy at Rugby when inheriting a large fortune from Mrs Helen Bostwick, widow of Jabez, one of the American Standard Oil millionaires, following a legal fight in the United States over her $29.25 million estate. His grandfather, Jabez, a founder partner of the company, along with the likes of the Rockefellers, had earlier died while trying to save his thoroughbred horses in a stable fire.

Francis had been an international level fencer and athlete and champion horseman in the army before turning to golf and achieving further distinction. An England golf international and winner of both the Dutch and Swiss Amateur titles, inter alia, perhaps his greatest achievement was in finishing 28th in the 1937 US Masters at Augusta. Rounds of 77, 74, 75, 76 gave him a total of 302, just two strokes behind Gene Sarazen and four in arrears of Sam Snead. Francis actually bettered the legendary American amateur Bobby Jones by a single stroke with the Green Jacket being donned by Byron Nelson. Francis also won the Silver Medal for leading amateur at the Open Championship on two occasions.

It had been in 1929 that the young Lieutenant Francis Francis of the Royal Horse Guards met and fell in love with Solveig 'Sunny' Jarman, the 'platinum blonde' music hall comedienne. He was introduced to the 19-year-old Norweigan/American actress while she was appearing in 'Hold Everything' at the Palace Theatre in London. The couple were engaged quickly and quietly. They married shortly before Christmas that same year in a ceremony conducted in strict secrecy at Christ Church in London. Less than a dozen friends attended, it was reported, and there were no bridesmaids. Lieutenant Francis duly resigned his commission under the tradition at that time that forbad officers from marrying actresses.

The old rule, dating back to the days when actors and actresses were classed with rogues and vagabonds, stated that officers intending to marry must inform the colonel of his regiment for approval. In the case of Francis, disapproval was taken for granted. Not surprisingly, the affair created a huge furore among the theatrical profession who by then had been accepted into society.

Francis was an even keener aviator than a sportsman. He had logged up 1500 hours of flying at the start of World War II in which he was to play a significant, though silent, role. His position as Commander FF of No 1 Ferry Pool of the Air Transport Auxiliary at White Waltham, near Reading, was a matter of public record. Only a handful of people, however, knew at the time that he was personally paying for the construction of fighter aircraft to sustain Britain's war effort.

Francis, who owned four chic London night clubs in the 1940s, recognised the design genius of James Martin and invested in Martin-Baker, a company which has endured to this day having achieved fame as inventors and manufacturers of the ejection seat.

Francis and Sunny had built a vast red-brick mansion on the shores of Lake Geneva in the tiny village of Gland between Geneva and Lausanne. Its Norweigan style steeply angled roofline contrasted with the most lavish of French modern interiors.

But Francis was to marry a second time and to another young actress from the London stage. His life subsequently switched from the glamour of London and European society to a form of wealthy frontier existence in the Caribbean. He and his new bride, Patricia Leonard, bought and developed from scratch an island from his half sister, Barbara 'Joe' Carstairs, who was known variously and exotically as 'the fastest woman alive', as the 'Queen of Whale Cay' and, most notoriously perhaps, as a long-time lover of none other than Marlene Dietrich.

We are getting a long way from birdies and bogeys but it is a journey worth taking as an insight into the society arm of the golfing body in the first half of the 20th century. At any rate, Francis built a custom-designed driving range at his home on Bird Cay as a practice area for himself and an eclectic bunch of visitors, among whom included Belgium's King Leopold III, the Duke of Windsor, Rock Hudson, Noel Coward, Greta Garbo and David Niven, friends all.

When the English Golf Union came to find a replacement for Francis Francis it knew it need look no further than Tom Thirsk. As the *Hull Daily Mail*, admittedly a big fan, commented, "he has never refused when he has been asked to play for his country, no matter how inconvenient it was."

Thirsk might well have been otherwise occupied that week. He had come within a whisker of gaining selection for the Great Britain and Ireland team to play United States in the Walker Cup, it being generally accepted that a victory against Scottish international Gordon Peters in the Amateur Championship earlier that year would have done the job. As it was, Peters prevailed narrowly to secure his passage on the boat to the States.

The solid Yorkshireman, whose preferred attire was a tie and comfortable cardigan, perhaps even with the occasional hole in the elbow, might have appeared a world apart from the inveterate socialite that was Francis. But the pair were friends, not just England international teammates and, in the case of one international against France, playing partners. It is known, by way of clear evidence, that Thirsk went straight from Baden-Baden to Chateau Solveig on Lake Geneva for a short holiday.

Thirsk was born in 1900 into the new money that grew from the industrial revolution.

"We were always told that Grandpa was born with a silver spoon in his mouth and he got bathed in milk," his granddaughter, Nicky Helyer, recalls.

"The family home was a beautiful house in Bridlington called Anglos. It is now a nursing home. We visited our grandparents for tea every Sunday. It was always cricket in the garden and pink gin in the evening. Grandpa would have his pink gin and the children would be given something like Ribena and water to look like his drink. He was a diabetic and we would pinch his diabetic wine gums.

"He was very much a family man. I never remember him

without his moustache. He used to tickle me with it. I would let out a little squeal of excitement. He was very cuddly. Grandpa ran a family flour mill business started by his father and uncle. It was passed on to Peter, one of Grandpa's twin sons. The business eventually closed down about 20 years ago and the mill was ultimately demolished."

The Thirsk family were Yorkshire through and through. James Thirsk, Tom's grandfather, who had learned his trade in the mid-1800s at Gordon Mills in Aberdeen, milled at first at Beverley Westwood then the Anglo-Hungarian Mills at Pocklington. The family purchased Station Mills at Nafferton in 1904 to be run by the sons, Thomas and David, Tom's father. Nafferton Mill, one of the longest surviving inland mills in the North of England, was what was known as a four sack plant, operating about three days a week. By the 1930s it had become a 13 sack plant, running day and night and providing employment for a large number of people in the area.

Thomas S Thirsk was what would be regarded as an upstanding member of the community, a long time East Riding County Councillor and stalwart of Pocklington Urban Council. He sat on the Flour Milling Control Committee during World War 1 and was a commissioner for the Inland Revenue in his district. David Thirsk, apart from being managing director of Messrs T S & D Thirsk Ltd, combined his leisure time between the Londesborough Lodge of Freemasons and Bridlington Golf Club where he was captain and known affectionately to everyone as 'Uncle David'.

The company supplied its award-winning Standard flour to Rowntree Mackintosh Ltd (previously Rowntree & Co Ltd) for use as an ingredient in the legendary Kit Kats as well as Smarties and Lion Bars. So, in a sense, both Francis and Thirsk might have been members of the Kit Kat Club...

Although his father introduced Tom Thirsk to golf at a young age, it was not always obvious that it would become his principle recreation. He had excelled in just about every sport he tried at school, finishing first or second in everything from throwing the cricket ball to all manner of running and jumping at Bridlington Grammar. He then moved to Sedburgh School, Cumbria's oldest and probably most distinguished public school, which, among many high-achieving former pupils, produced three England rugby captains in Wavell Wakefield, John Spencer and Will Carling.

Thirsk captained both the rugby and cricket teams at Sedbergh. Such was his prowess with bat and ball that he was invited to attend nets with Yorkshire County Cricket Club. The teenager had attracted attention with a school average of 102 and an outstanding all round performance for the Public Schools XI at Lords where he scored 81 and took 7 for 32.

Full-time cricket, however, was not for him. Thirsk joined the family firm straight from school, allowing him to combine learning the business, playing rugby for Hull and East Riding and establishing a formidable reputation as an amateur golfer.

He had broken the Bridlington course record at the age of 14. His real breakthrough year, which elevated him from a top County player to a contender at national level, was 1929. In that same 12-month period the 29-year-old lost in the final of the Yorkshire Championship, reached the last 16 of the Amateur Championship at Royal St George's and the quarter final of the English Amateur at Gosforth, and made his England debut in the international against Ireland at Royal Lytham.

The *Hull Daily Mail* golf correspondent wrote at the time: "He always had the polish. Now he has the recovery powers that stagger opponents, and now he is obtaining the experience that counts nearly 50 per cent in important events, he should continue to rise to the top flights. Not the least likeable thing about him is his disinclination to play to the gallery. He simply gets on with the job."

Thirsk was getting on with his real job. At t'mill, a situation which prompted the following comment from the *Hull Daily Mail*: "Thirsk's sportsmanship extends far beyond his attitude towards the game and an opponent. He has not much time for competitive golf these days for, as a married man with two young children, he has been devoting himself closely to the flour milling business of his father and uncle at Nafferton and his golf is confined to weekends and holidays."

He would have had to take a holiday in 1933 to represent England in the Home Internationals at Royal County Down. His twins, Peter and Paul (John), were born while he was on the famous Northern Ireland links. Thirsk duly dispatched Wilson Smyth of the host nation in the singles before withdrawing from the event. There followed a fast car journey, a ferry crossing to Heysham and a train back to Yorkshire. The journey took 16 hours but there to greet him were two healthy twin boys and a smiling wife.

By then he was Yorkshire champion and in demand for the many exhibition matches which would be arranged to open a new course and/or provide a showcase for visiting American professionals. One family photograph shows Thirsk marching jauntily down a Fulford fairway in the company of 11 time major champion Walter Hagen and his fellow globetrotter Joe Kirkwood, the first Australian to win on the PGA Tour in America.

A stylish swinger with a rare mastery of the little shot from off the green, Thirsk grew in stature until a point in 1937 that he was first chosen to captain England. The six-man team to meet France at St Cloud, Paris in the annual match included both Bentley brothers, Harry and Arnold, Thirsk's teammate in the Baden-Baden tournament.

Thirsk was being recognised as a leader as well as a fine player. This was confirmed later that year when Thirsk was named one of five selectors for the Great Britain and Ireland Walker Cup team the following year. GB&I had never won the biennial match against the United States and there was a determination to break the duck by introducing an element of professionalism. Not only were selectors primed to travel the length and the breadth of the islands to find the right players but they were also charged with arranging trials for the first time. The result was a famous first victory in 1938 at St Andrews. At least one well known commentator, clearly overcome by the occasion judging by the first paragraph of his report, was in no doubt about where most credit should be heaped.

"Let us now praise famous men," Berwick Law wrote. "We have done it; we have done it; we have done it at long last! The Walker Cup is ours for another two years at least and the long reign of terror is over...The Walker Cup was, in fact, won by John Morrison, Cyril Tolley, T J Thirsk, Willie Torrance and H Dickson (the selectors) who made the feat possible."

Thirsk, who achieved 13 holes in one before packing away his clubs, continued playing golf for England until the war while juggling his responsibilities as a father of four young children and one of the principal figures in the family flour milling firm. He was to hold the positions of managing director and chairman prior to his retirement from business in 1975.

Thirsk had married Gladys Dewhirst at Sailcoates, Hull in 1926. "She was known as Fanny,' granddaughter Nicky recalls. "Granny Fanny! My mother hated that name. Granny died in 1964, just before I was born. I never knew her, obviously, but she had the reputation of being absolutely lovely, a nice and kind person.

"Grandpa remarried after that to a member of a well known Ganton golfing family. She was Granny Joan. He adored Granny Joan. I used to spend half terms with them. He was one of the very first to get a colour television. I hated boarding at Humnanby Hall near Filey. I was really homesick and would phone Grandpa a lot from there. Grandpa and Granny Joan spent a lot of time at Ganton. They would sit down for pre-lunch drinks at a table in the bay window of a room now known as The Thirsk Lounge. I was given sixpences to play the fruit machine and I would putt on the practice green in front of the clubhouse. I had no idea he was so accomplished. He did not talk about his achievements. He was very quiet and unassuming.

"There were cabinets full of trophies in his house. Although I knew he was passionate about golf, he never went on about it. My Dad, though, said that Grandpa's work just filled in time between rounds of golf. I think he had a good foreman. He certainly had a gardener called Nelson who was such a wonderful character that he was treated not like staff but part of the family. The same could be said for Grace, the maid. She was a kleptomaniac. But she was never let go despite stealing all the time. Grandpa also looked after all the mill workers.

"I suppose he must have had a competitive streak, given his golfing success. But it did not come across in his persona. He was so calm, so chilled, so laid back and so loving. He was unfailingly polite and I never heard him raise his voice. There were never any airs and graces with Grandpa. He was a real family man, a real anchor and rock for us in our nomadic existence in Africa.

"In the last few months of his life we were back in Britain, living just down the road from his nursing home. He was very poorly and had to go into care. I went and sat with him every day. We would chat and watch television together. Granny Joan had died by then. Grandpa was still bright and sharp-minded but he suffered from terrible bed sores and was in a lot of pain. My Dad was with him, holding his hand, when he died.

"It was heartbreaking but I know he had quite a life."

7

THE BENTLEY PLAYBOYS

The 'Bentley Boys' were amateur golfing legends, on and off the course. Nowadays, they would be known in some quarters as players, and not just in the golfing sense.

Harry, the older brother by four years, collected the more trophies, and again we are talking both on and off the course. But Arnold had his moments, as his son, Robert, testified almost with pride.

"I would not mind betting they got around," Robert Bentley said. "Mum used to accuse Harry of playing the field. Dad was a bit the same way inclined. He once came back to our place in Cleveland Square, London, sporting a black eye. Someone had thumped him. There was probably a woman involved. Mum used to say that she would have divorced him years ago if not for me.

"Uncle Harry was the real playboy. In fact, he was a member of The Playboy Club in London. Dad was also a member, I think. He took me gambling once when I was a kid and later I went to a couple of casinos when he and Harry were around. Dad liked the horses and the old football pools. Harry was much more the casino type with women around him all the time. Harry was very, very blunt. He called a spade a spade. He and mum never got on too well. There was one occasion in Le Touquet when basically mum threatened him with a knife. He told her what he thought of her and she did not like his rudeness. Nothing happened, of course. Dad just laughed it all off.

"Harry was married four times. No children, at least none sired by him. Dad had been married previously and fathered two children before he got hitched to my mother."

While Arnold was in Baden-Baden in August, 1936, teaming up with Tom Thirsk as the English pair contesting the Grand Prize of Nations, Harry was heading from Glasgow to New York on the ocean liner, Transylvania, as a member of the Great Britain and Ireland side for the Walker Cup at Pine Valley.

Henry Cotton, who was to win the Open Championship three times, had given Harry some coaching, describing his friend as "an industrious player and a terrific trier." Always pleased to help, Cotton had also offered some advice to the Walker Cup players. "Don't play any shots on board," he said, "as the swaying will upset your swing. And resist the temptation to play golf immediately on landing." It is not known whether or not the GB&I players followed his advice. We do know, however, that they sailed home the victims of a 10 ½ – 1 ½ drubbing.

Given the prominence of both Bentley brothers in amateur golf either side of World War II, it is not possible to write about one without the other. Both brothers were naturally talented golfers who were actively encouraged by their golf-mad father, 'Pa', as he was known by everyone at Hesketh Golf Club. Arnold Edwin Lewis Bentley, to give him his full name, could not have been prouder when in 1949 the club conferred Honorary Life Membership on him and his two sons at a memorable triple ceremony.

Bobby Bentley confesses to knowing little about the earlier life of his grandfather other than where he worked and lived. The house, at 55 Marshside Road, Southport, enjoyed a view of the Hesketh clubhouse from where the boys could spot their father leaving for home. They knew it would take him less than five minutes to walk in the door.

'Pa' was a commercial handler for the well-known lard

manufacturing firm of N Kilvert & Sons based in Trafford, Manchester. Bobby possesses a letter addressed to Private Bentley from the company promising to reinstate him after his demobilisation at the end of World War I. Harry Vernon Kilvert, the then managing director, was knighted in 1921 for his services to business and the community.

Harry Bentley was born in Manchester, Arnold in Southport. Both attended University School, the oldest independent in Southport on its closure in 1972. It had been a Day and Boarders school catering for about 150 pupils, many of whom were sons of Armed Forces personnel stationed abroad. Notable former pupils include Ronnie White, solicitor, RAF pilot and one of England's greatest amateur golfers, and Phil Kelsall, still today the Blackpool Tower ballroom organist. Neither Harry nor Arnold went to university.

"Harry was the one who got the ball rolling when he founded H G Bentley Ltd, paper merchants," Bobby said. "My father was basically a lackey for his older brother at the time. But the two brothers got on very well. Each knew each other's strengths and weaknesses. They were very compatible in business and Dad blended into the firm. His job was often to entertain clients, perhaps take them to boxing matches. His outgoing personality was perfect for the role.

"Dad would spend the week down in the London office and come straight to the golf club on his return. That never pleased mum who used to refer to Hesketh as 'The Imperial Palace.' "

The company office was at 55 Park Lane and the company flat at No 166. And just along the road was the Dorchester Hotel where the brothers kept a permanently reserved table in the bar. There they would entertain and have meetings with clients such as Rowntree's – a customer of Tom Thirsk's company as well, as it happened – Terry's and Greenshields Stamps.

A letter from H G Bentley's accountants in reply to Bobby notifying them of his father's death fondly remembered the annual audit. "It was always a particularly enjoyable audit," the writer commented. "At least once or twice during the week or so that I was there, we would go to the Dorchester Hotel in Park Lane, via the back door, through the kitchens and into the lounge to have a few gins and tonic, followed by lunch." Nice work if you can get it.

Harry was the better golfer, certainly according to results, though Arnold's supporters would argue that but for the intervention of the war he might have matched his elder brother. Harry's victories included one English Amateur Championship, three Lancashire Amateur Championships, four German titles, the French and the Monte Carlo Amateur twice each and one Italian national success. Meanwhile, he held course records at various times at Royal Birkdale, St Anne's Old, Hesketh, Ormskirk, Le Touquet in France and both Bad Ems and Marienbad in Germany. His list of memberships was no less impressive - the Royal and Ancient, Royal St George's, Sunningdale, Hesketh and Monte Carlo.

He played for Lancashire on 42 occasions and represented England 58 times between 1931 and 1954. He also played in the 1934, 1936 and 1938 Walker Cup sides, his last appearance coinciding with Great Britain & Ireland's first success against the United States. He went on to become Chairman of the Selectors for the Walker Cup in 1953 as well as British Seniors Captain in 1967.

Harry was one of a group of leading amateurs, including Henry Longhurst, who travelled around the continent in the 1930s on a sort of golfing 'grand tour' headed by Brigadier-General AC Critchley as provider of the transport in his famous luxurious caravan. The Canadian-born Critchley, father of Bruce, the Sky Sports golf commentator and journalist, inter alia, was one of those filthy rich larger-than-life Marmite characters who totted up an eclectic mix of experiences and achievements, from wounded war hero and short-time Conservative MP to developer of the White City Stadium and founder of the Greyhound Racing

Association. Loved by his devoted friends, he was nevertheless not everyone's French martini.

Harry Bentley was also a 'character', albeit on a less grand scale than Critchley. The aforementioned Longhurst, best known as a distinguished BBC Television golf commentator and Sunday Times columnist, included a chapter on Bentley in his book, *It Was Good While It Lasted*.

Longhurst wrote of his friend: "Harry is one of the characters of the game. His home is in Southport and he has all the dourness of the Lancastrian. Underlying it is a penetrating dry humour, and that devastating frankness with which the North so often shocks the sheltered South. His accent, naturally broad, varies according to the company.

"Set him down in Mayfair among the up-twirled moustaches of the guardees and the futile chatter of the hothouse butterflies with nothing in life to do and too long in which to do it, and Harry will lay on a Lancashire accent with a trowel. He knows it amuses them. What they don't know is that it amuses him more.

"In search of business, golf and other forms of pleasure, Harry must have been to France 20 to 30 times. His French accent remains indescribably, and I think deliberately, atrocious, and his literal translations are enough to break the grammarian's heart. 'Un petit morceau de tout droit' for 'a little bit of alright' is nothing to him."

Longhurst delighted in telling how Bentley faced a tricky putt on the 18th green to keep alive his quarter final tie against 'Critch' in the French Amateur Championship at Biarritz. It was a one-in-twenty putt across a slope and onto a separate tier. Bentley interrupted his routine, stood upright and drawled the words "tres difficile" to the delight of the spectators before resuming position and holing the putt. The Lancastrian eventually won the match at the 21st on the way to retaining his title. Thereafter, he called France "my country" and the French "my people".

In fact, Harry would spend his later life in the south of France playing much of his golf with Bobby Halsall, the Royal Birkdale professional from 1945 to 1979. Halsall had managed to negotiate an enviable deal with his employers whereby he could spend the winter teaching at Monte Carlo Golf Club. Halsall died only a few years ago at the ripe old age of 99. Harry, a lifetime heavy smoker, passed away at his home in France in 1991 aged 84.

Longhurst noted that Harry employed a "painstaking, artificial swing" which would have turned heads for the wrong reasons. He was also a distinctly short hitter for his category of hitter. But he boasted a great short game and was a hard man to beat in match play.

"Harry's directness of thought and the disconcerting way in which he translated it into speech were never shown better than one sunny day in August a week or two before the declaration of war," Longhurst wrote. "The scene was the balcony of the golf club up on the hills behind Bad Ems, and Harry had just won the German championship. He had weathered the ordeal of having his hand pump-handled up and down by the golf dictator Karl Henkell, while the latter delivered himself of a long, unintelligible speech in German, and he had duly received the big silver trophy. It was a time when one crisis succeeded another, and talk of war was naturally in the air.

"'Would you like to take the cup home with you or would you rather leave it here?' Herr Henkell asked him.

"'Oh,' said Harry with brutal bluntness, 'I'll take it home. We may be at war before long.'

"Henkell…said there would be no war.

"'Never mind. You never know, and I'll take it just the same. If you win, you'll get it back anyway. And if we win, I'll keep it until we play for it again.'"

There is on display at the Golf Museum in St Andrews a letter dated 17th August 1939 – just 17 days before the outbreak of World War II – from the German Golf Association giving permission for Harry Bentley to take the German Amateur Trophy out of the country.

Like Harry, Arnold played much of his golf on the continent, primarily in France. Unlike Harry, Arnold stayed in England, taking over as managing director of the family firm when his older brother retired. Arnold, too, maintained multiple golf club memberships, in his case at the Royal and Ancient, Royal Birkdale, Royal Wimbledon and, of course, Hesketh.

Although the names of both Bentleys monopolise the honours boards in the splendid Hesketh clubhouse, it was Arnold who maintained the stronger link with his home club. The routine was for Arnold – and his paunch – to hold court at the bar from late afternoon to mid-evening and dinner…when not given to the dog.

Derek Holden, the Honorary Life President of Hesketh Golf Club and an ex-President of the Lancashire Union of Golf, played many a round with Arnold and, despite being a generation younger, spent many an hour in his company.

"Latterly, he played golf on a Saturday," Derek said. "He played in competitions now and again, perhaps the Easter Tournament and on occasion scratch medals. He would stand at the bar every night between about 4.30 and 7.30 surrounded by a group of about 20 to 30 people. Arnold was not a raconteur, stories needed to be dragged out of him. But as a most distinguished golfer, he commanded great respect and would be asked about all manner of subjects.

"He was not that forthcoming. There would certainly be no boasting about his achievements. He was definitely opinionated on national and government issues. He was a most personable companion, an avid reader of the *Daily Telegraph* who seemed to have committed much of it to memory before appearing for his regular evening pre-dinner tipple."

Bobby, his son, was familiar with the scene and the subjects.

"He was vehemently anti-Labour. God, he pontificated about politics. Dad used to listen to the various views on the topic of the day then give his opinion, spread out his hands palms down and pronounce 'End of story, right?' And the discussion moved on."

Judging by an excerpt of a speech made to club members during the 1980s, provided by Holden, Arnold Bentley would have been regarded as the most grunting of male chauvinist pigs even by the standards of those times. Hesketh were preparing to turn their 'men-only' Smoke Room into a mixed lounge. Bentley was not best pleased.

"The proposed alterations will mean that ladies have the full use of four out of five rooms in the clubhouse and the men will have just the snooker room," he ranted. "It will not be long before the ladies request a mixed snooker night - and you must realise that that is the beginning of the whole club being mixed. We shall be completely surrounded by women.

"Ladies should appreciate that they are only Associate Members of Hesketh and they have no say, or shouldn't have, in the running of the club – and have NO RIGHTS only PRIVILEGES – and it seems to me that the privileges of 100 ladies by far exceed the rights of 400 men. This is monstrous. Gentlemen, this is Hesketh Golf Club NOT The Hesketh Ladies Social Club – let us keep it that way."

Bobby Bentley would categorise his mother and father as having been "hard drinkers". He said: "Mum was a pretty good match for him. He would have half a mild followed by several whiskies and ice. He held his liquor well. I would describe them as heavy social drinkers, not lushes. He did not roll down the road singing or anything like that. He drank a lot and seemed to get the car home in one piece." It is said that an R&A captain once fondly described Arnold as a "well-oiled Bentley" at a function.

"I would say Harry was a leader of the pack and Dad was a follower," Bobby said. "There was a sister called Joan who suffered from Down's Syndrome and lived to a good age. The brothers were very fond of her. Harry was more of a go-getter; Dad let things lie a bit. Dad used to love going to Dorset. I remember he fell in love with a house and in the end bought it. But he never moved into it. Harry would have done it up and sold it for a profit."

Arnold showed sufficient talent as a teenager to be selected by the England boys team in 1928, the same year he won the Ashton Trophy at St Anne's Old Links. He went on to represent Lancashire on 37 occasions between 1930 and 1954, losing only 10 matches. Perhaps his finest hour in an individual capacity came shortly before the outbreak of war in 1939 when he triumphed in the English Amateur Championship at Royal Birkdale. And like his older brother, he broke the odd course record as his career progressed, at, for example, Hesketh, Blackpool Squires Gate and Penwortham.

Arnold was approaching his peak as a golfer when war intervened. He had joined the RAF and learned to fly. Bobby, who became a pilot and then a flying instructor himself, is qualified enough to take a gentle poke at the ability of his father in the cockpit.

"The RAF trained him to fly tiger moths – he was just not very good at landing them. Apparently, he put two quite rapidly on their noses. He told Mum he never saw any action because he was too old and, consequently, he was sent to Canada to grow tomatoes!"

In fact, a good number of RAF personnel were sent to Canada to train pilots and, specifically, to Ontario, one of the largest tomato growing areas in the world, to keep the crops going. The huge Heinz Corporation expanded into Canada by moving into an old tobacco factory in Leamington, Ontario as far back as 1909.

Henry Cotton had also joined the RAF, spending much of his time organising charity golf exhibition matches in aid of the Red Cross. Cotton, who received an MBE for his efforts in this area, more than once used the Bentley brothers as opposition for his fellow golf professionals.

Arnold represented England in the annual international against France in the three years immediately prior to the outbreak of World War II and 30 years on he was selected for the British Seniors Team. Like Thirsk, Bentley's preferred golfing attire was a woolly cardigan and collar and tie. His swing was smooth and powerful, anchored to the ground by an unusually wide stance. His secret weapon – though the secrecy disappeared with every victim – was a hickory shafted putter allied to a deadly putting stroke.

Bobby admits to having learned a great deal more about his father from Derek Holden than he did from either the horse's mouth or his mother. "He was very laid back and did not talk about achievements," Bobby said. "He was modest about his golf. His philosophy was simple – go and play and if you win, great. You really had to drag things out of him. There was another reason for a lack of information. Golf was not talked about in our house. Mum would not have appreciated any golf chat. She never took up the game. She hated it. She got in a state because Dad was always at the golf course."

The death of his father in 1998 at the age of 86 prompted his son to present the Hesketh Club with some of Arnold Bentley's trophies. Bentley had 'lost' a great many along the way. It was perhaps typical of him that his golfing booty lay around his flat in London, uninsured and, at least on the face of it, unloved. Twice the flat was burgled and twice the silver was removed. The only ones to survive were the dusty and blackened cups stashed away in a cupboard under the stairs, including a couple of silver vases from Baden-Baden.

Today they adorn the Hesketh clubhouse as a reminder of someone who loved his golf, his golf club and the members who would gather at the bar of a late afternoon for what the Irish would call the 'craic'.

8

TWO DAYS IN BADEN-BADEN

The decidedly non-sporty Adolf Hitler visited the Berlin offic-es of Albert Speer in the spring of 1937 to admire the model of what was intended to be a new national stadium with seating for an astonishing 400,000 spectators. It was during this very public show of support for the project that Hitler declared: "In 1940 the Olympic Games will take place in Tokyo. But thereafter they will take place in Germany for all time to come, in this stadium."

This was proof – if proof be needed – that the originally doubting Führer, who needed to be persuaded by Goebbels of the propaganda value of staging the 1936 Berlin Olympics, considered the event a resounding success, a demonstration of the might of the German people and their innate ability to organise on the grandest scales.

There are those who maintained that Jesse Owens, with his four high profile gold medals in the sprints and the long jump, had single-handedly scuppered Third Reich plans to hijack the Games for propaganda purposes. It is true that the sight and sound of a stadium full of Germans cheering wildly the exploits of an American 'negro', as was the terminology of the era, would not have been in the advance planning of Goebbels and Co. It is equally true that Hitler was known frequently to have expressed his displeasure to his inner circle any time a black athlete climbed the top of the podium. He spoke of the "unfair physical advantage", these sportsmen enjoyed over "civilised whites".

Owens would have been well accustomed to such sentiment. He was born, raised and lived in racist and segregated America. He sat in the back of buses and was refused entry to hotels in city centres. The story about Hitler refusing to shake the hand of Owens may have been myth but there was no denying the antipathy towards Owens from the ruling Nazis. Yet, according to one report in the London evening newpaper, *The Star*, there was another side to the gold medal which illustrated how a black man subjected to a daily life of racism might welcome a gesture of kindness, even an insincere one.

Roy Moon, a *Star* reporter in Berlin, wrote: "I was talking to Owens yesterday when word was received from the authorities that Herr Hitler had given permission for the coloured American to use the special tunnel into the stadium reserved for Hitler's use. Owens considered it a great favour for no-one other than Hitler and his bodyguards are allowed to use the tunnel."

The fact remains that Germany enjoyed a hugely successful Olympics, both in terms of champions crowned, medals won and logistical mastery.

"The main stadium... was expanded to accommodate 110,000 spectators, while the open-air swimming and diving pool seated 18,000," David Miller wrote in *The Official History of the Olympic Games and the IOC*. "The transport system, ferrying competitors from the excellently appointed men's Village... and the special guest houses for over 300 women competitors , was near fault-less. The electrical timing and photo-finish cameras were the most proficient yet used, the public address system audible to the point of intimidation, the Unter den Linden, Kurfurstendan and every main street were lined with huge swastika banners. Every café and restaurant had a radio blaring military music or proclamations of fealty to the Chancellor. Some 150,000 visiting foreigners could not fail to be impressed unless they paused to consider the ulterior motive of the extravagance on view. The opening ceremony was more like a coronation than a sports celebration, an ear-splitting fanfare greeting the arrival of the Führer."

By the closing ceremony, even the most ardent critics of the Nazi regime, who expected the Games to be used for propaganda purposes, conceded success. William Shirer, the celebrated journalist and war correspondent responsible for the text-book rated *The Rise and Fall of the Third Reich* remarked: "I am afraid the Nazis have succeeded with their propaganda. First the Nazis have run the Games on a lavish scale never before experienced, and this has appealed to the athletes. Second the Nazis have put up a very good front to the general visitors, especially the businessmen."

The actual competition brought Germany 89 medals, including 33 gold, to knock the United States off the top of the table for the first time since the Games were resurrected in 1896. This, remember, was despite the fact that Germany had been excluded from the Games of 1920 and 1924. USA finished second with 24 gold out of 56 medals (mostly on the track) while Great Britain managed just four gold from a total of 14 medals for 10th position.

The Winter Olympics had also been staged in Germany that year, at the Bavarian Alpine resort of Garmisch-Partenkirchen. Tiny Norweigan figure skater Sonje Henie became the star of the show by winning her third gold medal in a row before turning professional and gaining a huge following in the United States with her ice spectaculars. The highpoint for Britain, who won one medal each of gold, silver and bronze, was their shock defeat of Canada in the ice hockey final. That year saw the introduction of alpine skiing minus the presence of subsequent powerhouses, Austria and Switzerland, who objected to a ban on ski instructors. They were classed as professionals.

Germany finished second in the medal table with three golds and three silvers, albeit some way behind Norway and its seven gold, five silver and three bronze.

Der Angriff, the Nazi newspaper, reflected the sense of national glee after the summer Olympics. "We can scarcely contain ourselves for it is truly difficult to endure so much joy. If one may be permitted to speak of intoxication of joy then every German may be said to have reeled with happiness. It was also surprising for we had not reckoned with so many gold medals and so many victories. It is an odd but familiar experience and once again we have discovered after sturdy struggles what reserves are contained in us."

It ought not to have been so much of a shock. Their team of supposed amateurs had been financed for a year previously to attend special training camps in the Black Forest. And it was to the Black Forest that sports enthusiasts turned their attention post-Olympics as Nazi Germany tried to prolong the feeling of national pride. To specifically Baden-Baden, the chocolate box spa town in the south west of the country near France and Switzerland.

Baden-Baden in 1936 was still very much a destination for old money, English as much as German, a genteel holiday location for gentlemen and ladies who would while away the hours walking through the rose-scented English-style parks (you had to pay for access to these gardens), taking the waters and playing the odd game of chemin de fer at the famous Kurhaus Casino, the oldest in Europe. The Kurhaus Casino was to host the XIth Olympic Congress in 1981 – when delegates voted for Calgary and Seoul respectively to stage the 1988 winter and summer Games – and a historic NATO summit in 2009 attended by Barack Obama.

European society columns were sprinkled with news of toffs heading to the German spa town. *The Times* told us, for example, the vital information that "The Earl and Countess of Abingdon arrived in Baden-Baden yesterday and will be away from England for about a month" and that "the Hon Mrs Ronald Greville leaves England tomorrow for Berlin and then goes to Baden-Baden for the cure."

Fast forward 70 years to the modern newspaper equivalent

informing its readers that Elen Rivas, then girlfriend of Frank Lampard, treated Baden-Baden nightclub revellers to a table-top dance and rendition of 'I Will Survive', just about the most in-appropriate song for either WAGS (wives and girlfriends) or an English football team at the World Cup. The England players were billeted at Hotel Buhlerhohe, aptly the second best hotel in town.

Neat and compact Baden-Baden today, having survived unscathed both the Allied bombing of the World War II and, perhaps less comfortably, the Jagerbomb-drinking of the afore-mentioned sweethearts, still provides for the visitor an elegant mix of riverside walks, classical sculptures, high-quality museums and cream-cake architecture. Still going strong is the tennis club, the oldest in Germany, which was founded by English clergyman the Reverend Thomas Archibald White. The busy vicar also estab-lished a football club in the area as well as having a role in the foundation of the golf club, the third oldest in the country.

Having tried and failed to persuade the IOC to include golf on the official Olympic schedule, the German Sports Ministry came up with the idea of staging that triple addendum of golf, tennis and horse racing – society sports all – at Baden-Baden in the wake of Berlin 1936. Officialdom described the tournament as the most important in the history of German golf in a letter to the Mayor of Baden-Baden. The 'Heil Hitler' sign-off would have ensured that the local council never hesitated in forking out the requested 5,400 Reichmarks fee for the privilege of playing host.

The horse racing tied in with the big Iffezheimer race weekend. The tennis was won by Great Britain with E C Peters and J S Olliff defeating in the final the Yugoslav Davis Cup pairing of D Mitic and F Kukeljevic 6-2, 7-5. The Englishmen had already seen off in an earlier round the Germans H Henkel, subsequently the 1937 French Open champion, and H Denker.

But it was the golf which attracted the most local attention, pri-marily due to the fact that Hitler himself had donated the trophy.

91

Although it cannot be stated categorically that no British journalist covered the tournament, it seems unlikely. This was at a time when very few sports journalists travelled abroad, fewer still for the purposes of reporting on golf. There was also the clash with the Walker Cup match in America, a much higher profile event which would have attracted the interest of any golf correspondent able to persuade his editor to stump up for the trip. There was, too, a pretty universal reluctance to support anything arranged by the Nazi regime, official Olympics excepted. Remember, 36 countries had been invited to the golf in Baden-Baden and only half a dozen joined the host nation.

There was no question, though, that as far as the Germans were concerned this was an Olympic event. Flags were raised at the opening ceremony and at the trophy presentation; anthems were played and medals were presented. The winners were even given fir trees in a mirror of the Berlin Games which saw each gold medallist receive an oak. Owens collected a mini-forest. One he gave to his alma mater Rhodes High School, Cleveland, one flourished in his mother's home in Cleveland and one stands to this day among the cherished monuments of All American Row at Ohio State University. The fourth one died.

The golfers themselves seemed not to dispute German attempts to paint their tournament in Olympian gloss: Arnold Bentley, for example, wrote in pencil the words 'Olympic Games 1936' on each of his four cards.

The closing ceremony in Berlin took place on Sunday the 16th of August. That same day Owens was suspended by the American Athletic Union for taking an unauthorised – and presumably paid – 'run-out' on a scheduled trip to Sweden with the US track and field stars.

On the evening of Friday the 21st of August, Captain Wolfgang Fuerstner, the partly Jewish officer who had masterminded the Olympic village, left prematurely an Olympic farewell dinner, citing ill health. He returned home, put a gun to his head and shot himself. Fuerstner, a military man through and through, literally could not live with his impending dismissal from the army, a fate befalling all Jewish soldiers. Within hours of the Games ending the anti-Jewish signs that had been removed prior to the Olympics were put back again.

The sporting week in Baden-Baden began on August 23rd with two days of an international triangular golf match involving teams from Germany, France and Holland. German radio broadcast coverage of their own national team defeating Holland 6-3 and losing 4-5 to France who also trounced the Dutch 8-1. The final of the tennis took place on the 24th, the same day that Hitler announced the doubling of the length of conscription from one year to two, increasing in a single declaration the size of the army from 600,000 to 800,000

The Grand Prize of Nations took place over two days from the 26th using a format that was to be successfully employed by the Canada Cup then the World Cup from the 1950s into the 21st century – namely 72 holes of strokeplay with the combined score of the two-man teams determining the winner.

England (a distinctly non-Olympic denomination) would have been favourites not so much due to the strength of its team as the weakness of the opposition. France – who fielded their own Amateur Champion in Michel Carlhian and his teammate Jacques Leglise, who would go on to win the title the following year – deserved a prominent position in the reckoning. The hosts, still very much a fledgling country at international level, would not really have been considered.

In 19-year-old Leonard von Beckerath, however, Germany had a promising youngster who had already played for his country at senior level and would in 1938 win his own Amateur Championship. The previous year saw him lose in the final to none other than Harry Bentley, Arnold's older brother, having disposed of

Henry Longhurst in the quarter final.

Longhurst, who described Beckerath as 'possibly their best amateur up to that time', remembered the occasion well – and with obvious discomfort – in his 1971 autobiography *My Life and Soft Times*.

"I found myself three down with seven to play, accomplished the next four holes in 3,3,5,3, – and got nothing back," Longhurst wrote. "Three down and three to play. The par of the last three was 4,3,4 and I swear I did them in 3,2,3 and won the lot, including the 18th with a putt of ten yards. Von Beckerath beat me at the 20th but my finish was the topic of the day: 3,3,5,3,3,2,3! At least I had hauled down my colours in a modest blaze of glory and could look forward to something pretty heart warming in the *Evening Standard* (his employers)."

Von Beckerath came from a well known family of Mennonites who earned fortune and a measure of fame as musicians, artists, weavers, politicians, vintners, scholars and organ builders. Among the young golfer's antecedents were Adolf von Beckerath (1834-1915), a wealthy merchant and art dealer who became a connoisseur of the Italian Renaissance and boasted the finest collection of Dutch Masters in Germany. Alfred (1901-1978) was a celebrated composer and conductor who worked at the Theater der Jugend in Munich after World War II.

Earlier the great composer Johannes Brahms became a regular visitor to one of the Beckerath family country estates. Music would fill the air with Brahms seated at a piano accompanied by the female Beckeraths on violin, viola and cello. The maestro is reputed to have exclaimed: "Holy Cow, one has to be on his toes to play with this crowd!" Meanwhile, Willy von Beckerath dipped into his crayon box to draw the iconic portrait of Brahms at the piano.

Leonard von Beckerath, the son of Oskar, a factory owner in Krefeld, the so-called 'velvet and silk city' near Dusseldorf, had his first golf lesson from a professional in 1933, the year he began a long association with Krefelder GC. His son, Aurel, retells a family tale about that a lesson that was shared with his sister.

"It was said about my aunt that she showed enough to suggest she could become a fairly good golfer," Aurel von Beckerath says. "The professional told my father that he had the makings of a decent lumberjack."

Within a year, however, he had made his debut for the senior German team, the first of 20 international appearances between 1934 and 1956. (Germany did not play many international matches in those days and none, of course, during the War.)

Aurel was born in 1963 by which time his father had reached the age of 46. "He was really more of a big brother and an adviser than a father to me. He was very blunt. He meant what he said and he said what he meant. And when he had finished speaking, that was it. He would cut a telephone conversation dead or if face to face just turn round.

"But he always helped people when they needed help. Not necessarily with money. For example, if you needed picking up in the middle of the night he did it without question. He was very supportive of me in my schooling and my career and he did not mind that I did not join his business retailing protective foil."

Like Thirsk, his English opponent, Beckerath was a terrific all round sportsman. A highly accomplished mountaineer, he was involved in German expeditions to K2 and the so-called Pakistan 'killer mountain' Nanga Parbat, the ninth highest in the world, as well as reaching base camp at Mount Everest. Beckerath was also an excellent skier, both on snow and on the water. If the speed and daring of his driving did not graduate to competitive racing, it certainly left a mark on his son who described it in scarily graphic fashion. "The gap between his front bumper and the rear bumper of the car he overtook on the motorway measured the same as the Saturday edition of the *Frankfurter Allgemeine Zeitung.*"

Just recently, a Porsche red 901 (chassis No 57) which he once owned, hitherto the last of 82 to be traced, was found rotting at the back of a farm building. It is now in the Zuffenhausen Porsche Museum in Stuttgart undergoing a complex reconstruction.

The junior in the German team at Baden-Baden in terms of experience, Beckerath proved the senior in performance. But Carl Alexander Hellmers, at 39 twenty years older than his teenage teammate, was no mug. Hellmers had won the German Amateur Championship back in 1924 and had represented his country on 34 occasions by the time war broke out. He went on to become twice German Senior Amateur Champion during the 1950s.

A club obituary talks about former president C A (as he was known) Hellmers dying on September 11, 1988 in his 92nd year. "Herr Hellmers," it goes on, "was a very well known personality, far beyond Falkenstein. His whole life was devoted to golf. For 32 years, C A Hellmers was active in various leading positions in the club. He founded the club newspaper and sustained it for 16 years after his retirement. With unwavering commitment and interest, he shared his golf knowledge with the members. For him, Falkenstein was a sacrosanct paradise."

The same club newspaper had printed a eulogy to C A on the occasion of his 75th birthday from an old friend. It gives a flavour of Hellmers' character, his golfing prowess and the fondness with which he was held. The writer used the form of an open letter to urge his friend to write a definitive history of German golf.

"Certainly you would have to curb somewhat your priceless gift of embellishing true experiences into not quite so true anecdotes, but with your diligence, your accuracy and your presentation skills, this would be a most worthwhile read for any German golfer... The fact that you dare not risk playing any more due to your lumbago strikes me as sad. How I would have wished to see again your rhythmic swing with the somewhat hunched left shoulder and follow your shot, albeit not as long as before, as it splits the fairway... It was Goethe who said, 'The person who has made the best of their own time has lived for ever.' Now, to whom could this apply more than to you? Even if you're not playing at the moment, your life remains rich. You follow our sport with undiminished interest... Even in old age, life can be good, and it is the heartfelt wish of all German golfers that this remains the case for you for a long time to come."

Hellmers survived the war; Beckerath survived the Russian front. But only just, according to his son.

"Leo was a 21-year-old lieutenant at the end of his national service when the unbelievable and sad time started," Aurel said. "He told me he was a motorcycle rider with the cavalry in Northern France and then much further away in Russia."

It appears likely that Beckerath was captured during the Battle of Moscow and sent to a prisoner of war camp, one of three million German POWs held by the Soviet Union during World War II. Soviet figures suggest that nearly 400,000 German POWs died in the camps run by the NKVD (the People's Commissariat for Internal Affairs), though Germany puts the number at around a million.

"Father spent almost seven years as a POW. One day in 1947 he turned up in Rheinland-Pfalz at a mill my great grandmother had bought in 1929. He was suffering from severe hunger swelling brought on by starvation. He had swollen legs, a bloated belly and was barely able to crawl. It took him almost a year to regain his health and be fit enough to return to his home town of Krefeld."

It appears that Baden-Baden was chosen for the Olympic addendum more for the beauty of the location, the existence of a racecourse and the history of the tennis club than the excellence of the golf course. Carved out of the forest, meandering through glades in and out of open undulating countryside, it was more renowned for its scenery than as a fair test of golf. The course, which measured an incredibly short 4,513 yards, featured ten par

3s of varying length, some of them devilishly difficult, three par 5s and five par 4s for a total par of 65. The quirky nature of the layout, however, made breaking 70 far from a straightforward task.

Tom Thirsk, in a letter home to his mother, described the Baden-Baden course as "short but tricky, with some of the holes the most peculiar I have ever seen." The peculiarity seems to have stemmed from the combination of changes in elevation, narrow fairways and tiny, sloping greens.

Certainly, the limited contemporary reports of the action described a catalogue of catastrophes with players taking a heavy sprinkling of 7s and 8s in part caused by a high instance of players four-putting.

Baden-Baden was in the sweltering grip of a heatwave that week. Thirsk was forced to remove his cardigan on occasion and roll up his shirt sleeves. Beckerath, meanwhile, had produced some pretty hot stuff in practice, a 62 according to the buzz in the clubhouse. Could the home team possibly get their hands on Hitler's trophy?

They started brightly. Rather, young Beckerath began well, reaching the turn in a best of the morning 34. Without walkie-talkies, computers or the all-seeing television cameras, what we have come to know as rolling news was provided by good old word of mouth. No-one needed to walk far from the clubhouse to see that Hellmers had started disastrously by requiring three shots to escape a bunker at the opening hole. He also lost a ball to be out in 40.

Both English players, independent of each other, fell foul of the notorious 8th green by four-putting. Bentley experienced one of those apparently frequent minor disasters by taking 7 at the 14th on the way to a 74. Thirsk came home in 34 for what proved a respectable 70.

Beckerath, too, found trouble on the inward half. But he gained compensation for a 7 at the 13th by holing a chip shot at the last for a birdie 2 and a round of 68. With Hellmers, in contrast, double bogeying the 18th for a 75, Germany posted a lunchtime total of 143. The hosts were level with England.

The temperature rose in the afternoon and, ultimately, fatigue set in. Not before Beckerath managed a best-of-the-day outward 32 to be followed closely by Thirsk's 33 and Hellmers's 34, including yet another 7 at the 4th. The journey home was short in yardage and long in torment. Hellmers took a ghastly 8 at the 16th where he lost two balls, yet still signed for a 72. His verdict was that he played well. Poor Bentley was keeping afloat well enough until the 14th where he added a 9 to a morning 7. A 6 at the same hole marred an otherwise steady 70 for Thirsk.

Halfway, 36 holes down 36 to go, and, to the surprise of not least the home nation themselves, Germany led England by five strokes with France a further five behind – respectively 282, 287 and 292.

Back home in Blighty, the Thirsk family gathered round the radio. The then 15-year-old Donald Bisland, who was to become Tom's son-in-law, recalled the scene in a letter to the family.

"I was on my summer holidays from Worksop College and I remember the occasion as if it were yesterday," he wrote. "For the four days we all – that is to say Great Grandfather David Thirsk (Tom's father), Tom's mother, Fanny Thirsk, my mother and father and I – sat round the radio at Westwood, David Thirsk's home on the Bridlington sea front, listening to reports as they came in. It was more than exciting."

The recollection is perhaps not entirely accurate. The tournament did not last four days, only two. Donald also got several dates wrong. There was no Radio 5 Live around at that time. There would not have been hourly or even occasional reports throughout the day. It is likely that Thirsk's family and friends had tuned into Radio Berlin which *The Times* of the 27th noted was broadcasting a report on the 'International Golf Tournament at Baden-

Baden' between 10.20pm and 10.30pm.

The second day dawned just as bright and warm as the first. Another day to leave the cardigans in the locker room for Thirsk and Bentley. For the Germans, the heat was on. But the pressure proved too great for the young Beckerath who found the burden of carrying his teammate too great. Beckerath played the first six holes of the third round in a calamitous six over fours. That he covered the remaining 12 in six under fours for a 72 was to his great credit. Yet again, Hellmers required 40 for the front nine in a 76.

England – and Thirsk in particular – went for the German jugular. While Bentley assembled a solid 70, Thirsk unleashed a spectacular 65, including an inward 30 comprising figures of 342, 443, 532. England had gone from five strokes behind Germany to eight ahead of the overnight leaders. According to one contemporary German report, Thirsk was noted for his "round, powerful swing and his naturally quick but never hasty play."

The same observer could not look at Arnold Bentley without thinking of his older and better known brother, Harry. "(Arnold) can be recognised even at a distance as the brother of our earlier master. (He has) the same stance, with the head pivoted forward, and he wears the same striped shirts and on the left hand the same glove. He is not the same class as his brother. He is somewhat more nervous and does not have the gift of the great Harry to free himself from a difficult situation or a difficult lie."

If there was to be another swing of the pendulum in Germany's favour, there needed to be a fast start from Beckerath. It was not to be. The teenager turned in 41 and it was only pride which saw him come home in 31 for a 72 which secured third place. Hellmers could do no better than 73.

Thirsk was again superb. Having reduced the back nine to 30 in the morning, Yorkshire's finest covered the front nine after lunch in 31 imperious blows on the way to his second 65 of the day.

The *Hull Daily Mail* enthused about Thirsk "at his golfing great-est", adding "he has never played so superbly... (He) undoubtedly secured the tie for Britain, for Bentley, after a good 70 in the third round, fell away and returned 75 for the last."

Bentley, exhausted by the heat and safe in the knowledge of victory, staggered over the line with a 6, 6 finish. England had triumphed with a total of 562, four ahead of France who were another eight in front of Germany. The Hitler Trophy, as it was christened many years later, was heading to England.

But first there was the presentation...

9

HITLER IN THE HUFF

As a golfer and the brother-in-law of Karl Henkell, the so-called 'Golf Führer', it was no surprise to see Joachim von Ribbentrop, Hitler's notorious foreign minister, at Baden-Baden for the Grand Prize of Nations.

Ribbentrop had been a regular visitor to – and keen patron of – Wannsee GC in Berlin where Peter Alliss's father Percy was the professional from 1926-32. The link with Henkell was forged when the future ambassador to Britain married Annelies, the sister of the heir to the sparkling wine empire. It was a union which provided the social-climbing Ribbentrop with money and position, two commodities distinctly lacking among the misfits of the Nazi Party.

Ribbentrop was, according to historian Laurence Rees, "the Nazi almost all the other leading Nazis hated". Goebbels notoriously said of him: "He bought his name, married his money and swindled his way into office." John Weitz, who wrote a biography of Ribbentrop entitled *Hitler's Diplomat*, described him as "a tennis-playing, well-groomed fellow with city and country houses, a well-born, well-dressed wife, and several handsome kids."

Like most of Hitler's closest associates, Ribbentrop was heavily involved in the Olympic Games. His appointment to the embassy in London having just been announced, he spent much of the fortnight entertaining members of the Anglo-German

Fellowship and those twin giants of the British press, Lords Rothermere and Beaverbrook.

By way of entertainment for foreign dignitaries and prominent Germans, Hermann Goering, Josef Goebbels and Ribbentrop – a Big Three if ever there was one – each threw a huge party during the Olympic fortnight. Ribbentrop was determined to win the gold medal for the most lavish. Six hundred people were invited to his family home in Dahlem, one of the most affluent areas of Berlin to the south west of the city. All guests were assigned Mercedes cars, driven by uniformed SS or men from the Nazi party's motor corps. A massive tent was erected to provide cover for the gardens and tennis court. Water lilies decorated the swimming pool and there were rhododendrons everywhere. Barnabas von Geczy, Germany's best band leader and a favourite of Hitler, was hired to play as the great and the good, the bad and the ugly sipped champagne and tripped the light fantastic.

Ribbentrop could not have been busier and his wife was about to give birth to a son they would name, with predictable obsequiousness, Adolf. It was precisely because Hitler himself had given the trophy for the Grand Prize – along with Ribbentrop's tie to Henkell and his liking for golf – that despite everything that was going on in his life, the chief toady headed for the Black Forest. He wanted to be there in case Germany won the event. Should that happen, he would take charge and claim the credit.

That looked possible at the half way stage with Germany holding a five-stroke lead. So, Ribbentrop telephoned Hitler that evening to float the idea of the Führer making a dash to Baden-Baden to present his own trophy to a couple of heroes of the Third Reich. He would not have committed himself to attending in person without knowing Germany were well placed.

It would have been too lengthy a journey from Berlin, some 500 miles away, on the roads of the day, with even a dawn start offering no guarantee of Hitler arriving in time for the prize-giving ceremony. However, immediately following the closing ceremony, Hitler, tired and weary from all the activities of the Olympic Games, had decamped for a holiday to his beloved country retreat at Berchtesgaden. Even the most evil of dictators needs to take a break from dictating now and then.

Hitler was a car enthusiast who actively enjoyed being driven about in his fleet of Mercedes vehicles. The 300-mile trip was just about manageable. He and his entourage could depart in the morning and stop for lunch on the way. There would have been an arrangement whereby Ribbentrop would either make contact during the day or, in extremis, intercept the convoy should the situation change. Hitler would not have wanted to risk the embarrassment, as he saw it, of presenting his own trophy to people he was planning to wage war against, especially not the English.

Ribbentrop was content. He would soon be a father again. At the end of October he and his family would arrive in London to take up his position as Ambassador to the Court of St James. His son, Rudolf, would be enrolled in Westminster School. Before that Ribbentrop would be promoted by Himmler to the rank of General in the SS as a special advisor to Hitler. The Führer may have called Ribbentrop "my little champagne salesman" to his face but there was no doubting his standing in the hierarchy. Ribbentrop enjoyed his status as a fully-fledged member of Hitler's inner circle, until that is he was hanged at Nuremburg on the 16th October, 1946.

As a trusted confidant, Ribbentrop could and would survive irritating Hitler from time to time. Still, Ribbentrop would not have enjoyed August 27th, 1936. News filtered back to him throughout the morning of Beckerath's disastrous start to the third round and of Hellmers's continuing problems with the front nine holes at Baden-Baden. It soon became apparent that England had caught up and overtaken the Germans with the French also in contention. By the end of the third round at lunchtime on the second day a German victory seemed unlikely. A disconsolate Ribbentrop knew he would have to either tell Hitler personally or get a message to him. He would have experienced often enough his leader's infamous temper.

Meanwhile, the mood in the English camp had shifted dramatically from despair to joy. No-one was happier with the morning turnaround than Major Tiny Lavarack, the secretary of the English Golf Union. By journeying to Baden-Baden, Lavarack had given an official stamp of approval to English representation in a tournament which, remember, was bypassed by all but six of the 36 invited countries. In so doing, Lavarack risked personal criticism from other members of the EGU and beyond.

Lavarack had been several times to Germany and was a personal friend of Karl Henkell. The pair, along with English Golf Union president, Major B C Burton, formed a troika in charge of the European Golf Association on its formation in 1937. A preliminary committee had been formed at Baden-Baden during the Grand Prize to discuss the establishment of the pan-European organisation of national federations. The EGA formally came into being on the 20th November 1937 at the clubhouse of the Golf-Club Grand Ducal de Luxembourg. The outbreak of war saw it lie dormant for 10 years until its re-formation.

Lavarack sent both Thirsk and Bentley telegrams on the opening day of the Baden-Baden competition. Thirsk's read: "Best of luck and a good day's sport, Tiny."

A 'good day's sport' for Lavarack and the English was delayed 24 hours. England, led by Thirsk with the first of a brace of stunning 65s on the second day, were rampant; the German team, inexperienced and not remotely of the same calibre as either the English or the French players, were in retreat. The expectation must have been overwhelming. Perhaps the teenage Beckerath, the star of the opening day, alerted to the arrival of the Führer, suffered from nerves, and understandably so. He was only

19, albeit already identified as Germany's most promising golfer.

Ribbentrop knew he had to take action. His driver was alerted, an official car readied and off Ribbentrop sped, as if in a car chase straight out of the film *Von Ryan's Express*. These war films always portray Nazi cars going like stink then flying over the edge of the road into a tree. Not on this occasion. Ribbentrop had to head Hitler off at the pass not drive into it. And so the two convoys met on the road from Berchtesgaden to Baden-Baden.

There would have been very few on hand to record the reception given by Hitler to his British Ambassador. There is little need for an eye witness account. We can well imagine that the notoriously bad-tempered Hitler flew into one of his notorious rages and delivered a venomous rant in the direction of Ribbentrop. Hitler would certainly have referenced the ineptitude of the trumped up champagne salesman. He might have threatened a posting to the Eastern Front when it eventually opened. The air would have turned as blue as a pair of Ayrian eyes. Before you could say 'Dummkopf', Hitler turned his cavalcade around and headed back to his country retreat. Or perhaps he struck out for Berlin to prepare for an annexation or two.

Whatever, the story was born that the Yorkshire/Lancashire combination of Messrs Thirsk and Bentley, England's cardigan-clad golfing storm troopers, forced Hitler to turn tail. It would be several years before that happened again.

But did it even happen that time round? Was the story born out of the imagination rather than based in fact? Did Hitler, anything but fresh from a fortnight of constant appearances during the Olympic Games, really embark on a 600-mile round trip to present a trophy for golf, a sport about which he cared not a jot? Was Ribbentrop at Baden-Baden in the first place and, even if he were, would he have dared to summon his Führer from one side of the country to the other?

The Germans think not. That is to say, those few Germans who have given the matter any thought at all think not.

"The story is complete rubbish," Christoph Meister, the pre-eminent German and Olympic golf historian, said. "Hitler had no interest whatsoever in golf, which he considered an elite Anglo Saxon sport. There is nothing in the archives to suggest he made the journey to Baden-Baden. It was a long way by car. The story was probably made up by the English. I do think Ribbentrop was at Baden-Baden, however."

The author received a reply from the German National Archive to a query about Hitler's movements for the week of the sporting festival in Baden-Baden. This following is a translation of a response written in German:

"I have to inform you that following investigations carried out in the Federal Archive in Berlin, no documentation can be identified confirming Adolf Hitler staying in Berchtesgaden and travelling to Baden-Baden after the Olympic Games. Included in these checks were existing resources R43 Reichs Chancellery and NS10 – the Personal office of the Führer/Chancellor."

A similar reply was received from the archives in Munich and Baden-Baden.

We have the aforementioned Tiny Lavarack to thank – if that's an appropriate word - for a story that received no coverage at the time and precious little over the eight decades since. As previously stated, there were no British journalists at Baden-Baden. German newspapers either did not send staff to the event or chose not to report the outcome. There is some suggestion that German radio were present and, in that regard, we know from Peter Thirsk's son-in-law that the family back in Bridlington gathered round Radio Berlin to listen to a broadcast.

There is, however, one key piece of documentary evidence in existence, albeit not a contemporary one.

It comes from a 1954 edition of *The Star*, one of London's

evening newspapers now long gone. In his column entitled, 'At The 19th Hole', Geoffrey Cousins wrote the following.

"Strange golf trophy which once made Hitler turn tail has just found a place in the Golfers' Club in Whitehall Court, within a wedge shot of Downing Street. It is a gilt metal salver given as a prize for an international foursome (sic) tournament at Baden-Baden in connection with the Olympic Games of 1936.

"The Golfers' Club, formed 61 years ago to provide a London meeting place for enthusiastic golfers, has been elected to life membership of the English Golf Union. To commemorate the election Major A Whitley Lavarack, EGU President, handed over the trophy. Afterwards he told me the story.

"Hitler, who had no interest in golf, agreed to present the trophy only if Germany won it. With one round to go this seemed certain (sic). The German pair led by three strokes, and Foreign Minister Ribbentrop and German GA President Carl (sic) Henkel (sic) sent a message telling the Führer it would be safe for him to arrive.

"Then the British pair, TJ Thirsk of Yorkshire and Arnold Bentley of Lancashire had a record round to win, and another message was sent to Hitler, then on his way from Berlin. He burst into a typical rage, ordered his car to return to the capital – and left a rather perturbed Henkel (sic) to present the trophy."

There are several inaccuracies in the story other than the spelling of Karl Henkell: it was a team strokeplay event, not a foursome; Ribbentrop was not appointed Foreign Minister until February, 1938; the German pair were eight strokes behind England (and one behind France) with one round to go, not three ahead; Hitler was coming from Berchtesgaden not Berlin.

Despite the factual errors, there is no way Cousins would have invented the story. Cousins was one of the most respected golf correspondents of his day. One of the founding members of the Association of Golf Writers, he served as secretary of the organisation from its inception in 1938 to 1963, treasurer from 1938 to 1952 and eventually President from 1976 to 1978. Cousins became a highly regarded golf correspondent for the Press Association.

"There is not a chance that Geoffrey would have made up the story," Renton Laidlaw, the distinguished golf writer and broadcaster, said. "He was as straight as they come, both as a journalist and a person."

Which is not to say that his source might not have been mischievously spinning a yarn. Everybody liked a good Hitler story in those days. Perhaps Lavarack supped from the bowl of hyperbole when recalling the events at Baden-Baden. Perhaps he even told 'the one about Hitler turning his car around' to the English players over a glass or two of bubbly during the celebrations. Perhaps a myth was born in the heady cocktail of victory and champagne. Perhaps he was just repeating one of those rumours which sprout from wherever and acquire arms and legs.

Both Derek Holden, friend and playing partner of Arnold Bentley at Hesketh, and Bob Bentley, Arnold's son, take a less Machiavellian view of events. Both, independently of each other, were told the Hitler story by Bentley and both see no reason to doubt the the veracity of his words. Holden, who became an integral figure in the story of the Hitler Trophy, is a firm believer.

"I remember Arnold telling me the Hitler story over dinner," Holden said. "I recall him using the phrase, 'bloody Germans'. He would occasionally talk about the Baden-Baden tournament in conversation with his friends when standing at the bar. But Arnold was very modest and did not like to speak about his victories.

"The only time he got excited about it was when an article appeared and got everything wrong. He would say: 'that's wrong, that's wrong and that's wrong,' pointing out the various inaccuracies. There was one report in the *Sunday Post* in 1986 which he wrote all over, correcting the errors.

"Significantly, though, he did not highlight any problem with the line that 'Ribbentrop raced off by car to intercept Hitler, and break the bad tidings.' And even more revealing, I think, he never disagreed with the headline on the story, 'So Hitler Went Off In The Huff'.

Bob Bentley grew up in a household where, perhaps surprisingly, there was little talk about golf. "Ma was a pretty impenetrable barrier," Bentley explained. "She did not like golf at all. She would freeze if it was mentioned. I was aware that Dad had won the German competition, but all he would say when I asked him about it was 'I don't know where the bloody trophy is.' Later, though, he told me about turning Hitler back. Like Derek, I recall the use of the phrase, 'bloody Germans'. I think he mentioned it only the once."

While Bentley mentioned it "once", according to his son, Thirsk appears not to have referred to the Hitler story at all. None of the cuttings from the local Yorkshire newspapers make any reference to the aborted car journey. And there is no word from Thirsk's son, Peter, about him being told that specific tale. Prior to his death Peter Thirsk became involved in researching the event and expressed both anger that the EGU had let go of the trophy as well as a desire for it to return to England. But there seemed to be a regret on his part that he had not spoken to his father about what happened in 1936.

"My father died in 1979," he wrote in an article for the magazine *Through The Green* in June, 2004, "and I regret not having had the opportunity to speak to him at length about this trophy. Being a modest man, he never spoke about his golfing successes."

This modesty very much ties in with the memories of Thirsk's two daughters, Nicky and Ginny, as well as his great granddaughter, Mel. None of the three has any recollection of Tom Thirsk mentioning the possibility that Hitler himself had been on his way to present his trophy.

"You always regret things you should have asked," Nicky Helyer said. "I was probably selfishly not interested at the time. I never asked at all about his golf when I was a schoolgirl. And he never mentioned it. Of course, I became aware of the Baden-Baden event when uncle Peter started to get interested."

The absence of any evidence from the Thirsk side of the England team supports the German view that the Hitler story is a myth or, if you prefer, a tall tale invented at a time when stories about the German bogey man abounded. Remember, Hitler, according to the ditty to the Colonel Bogey tune, "has only got one ball".

Kuno Schuch, the director of the German Golf Archives in Cologne, points out the lack of hard evidence. He and other golf historians have researched documents relating to Hitler's agenda that day and found nothing to indicate he jumped in a car and headed to Baden-Baden, let alone anything to suggest he turned around even more swiftly when learning of the English advance.

"There is nothing in the National Archive in Berlin and nothing in the diary kept by Hitler's secretary to say either that Hitler intended to go to Baden-Baden or decided at the last minute to head there," Schuch stated.

"My personal view is that after the success of the Olympic Games, he began preparing the way to conquer Europe and had no idea of going to Baden-Baden to present his own prize, whether Germany won it or not.

"I think the story is a myth. I think the English heard a rumour that Hitler was going to present the trophy and when he did not arrive, they made up their own story about him turning round in their disappointment."

Schuch conceded – just as Derek Holden insisted – that just as there is no firm documentary evidence to corroborate the story, there is equally none to give lie to it. Schuch takes the view that Hitler signed off on the event as a means of populist propaganda but took no interest in the tournament itself or the outcome.

"Golf at the time in German was an aristocratic sport, and Hitler wanted to present himself as a man of the people," Schuch says. "That's what his interest in the tournament was. It was a way of showing that he was trying to make an elitist game accessible to the masses."

The fact that nothing can be found is perhaps merely a reflection of the fact that so much was destroyed. It is also an indication that nobody looked too hard since it has been until fairly recently a national trait in Germany not to poke about in a past best forgotten. Lately, however, a younger generation has been encouraged to feel more comfortable about confronting the darker side of Germany's history.

Thomas Ihm, a noted radio journalist and member of Baden-Baden, makes an interesting point. "Germans of a certain age don't tend to look back," he told me. "They don't really do anniversaries because there are things they don't want to remember. Because the past was so bad, they only look forward."

Golf historian Albert Bloemendaal, who wrote an article on the Baden-Baden event for *Golfika*, the magazine of the European Association of Golf Historians and Collectors, bemoaned the lack of source material, declaring: "I have been researching in whatever source available. It was no surprise that there was not all that much. The developments in Germany in later years gave reason enough for not reminding us what happened there. In a way the Berlin Olympics were a beginning of something we would rather forget."

So do we believe the version of Tiny Lavarack as told to Geoffrey Cousins and of Arnold Bentley as related to his son, Bobby, and his friend, Derek Holden? Or do we prefer the lack of any documentary evidence in Germany, the difficulties presented by the logistics and the probability that Hitler might have been otherwise occupied with thoughts of world domination?

Or do we suspend belief and hitch our wagon to the version

PARIS 1900

GOLDEN COUPLE... Peggy Abbott and Charles Sands, the American winners of the first individual gold medals for golf

ST LOUIS 1904

CANADIAN CLUB MAN...
George Lyon, winner against
the odds at Glen Echo
Photos courtesy of Glen Echo Golf Club

GERMANY
1936

**A WALK IN THE
BLACK FOREST...**
Baden-Baden plays host
to the Hitler Trophy

WINNERS AND LOSERS...
Above, the English pairing of
Tom Thirsk and Arnold Bentley

Below: The Germans, teenager
Leonard von Beckerath and Carl
Hellmers

*Pictures courtesy of the German Golf
Archive, Cologne*

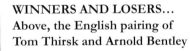

ENDURING CHARACTERS:
Arnold Bentley – and his scorecard
from Baden-Baden – and Tom Thirsk
in later years

Arnold
Bentley
at the
Liverpool Golfers
Captain Dinner
Adelphi
Hotel - 1965

CONTINUING THE JOURNEY... The Hitler Trophy passed from Leonard Sculthorp, the typewriter king of Glasgow, to Hesketh Golf Club on the Lancashire coast

GOLFPREIS DER NATIONEN
THE GOLF PRIZE OF THE NATIONS
Donated by Adolf Hitler

held at BADEN-BADEN GERMANY
in conjunction with the
BERLIN OLYMPIC GAMES 1936

WINNERS
ENGLAND: Arnold Bentley (Hesketh) & Tommy Thirsk (Bridlington)

PRIDE OF PLACE… The Hitler Trophy and Arnold Bentley's gold medal on display in the new dedicated room at Hesketh Golf Club

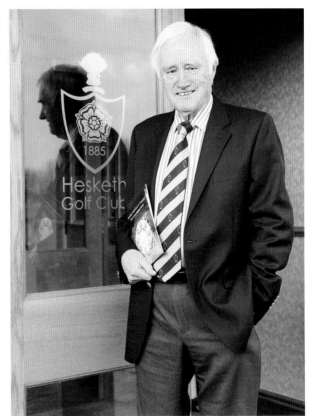

AT HOME IN HESKETH... Derek Holden, prime mover in bringing the Hitler Trophy to Hesketh and, below, the Hitler Tree, for which members reserved a special place and ritual...

RIO DE JANEIRO 2016

GREENS AND GOLD... The Brazilian setting for Jordan Spieth, Rory McIlory, Justin Rose et al to contest the newly restored Olympic golf tournament

of Tom Thirsk's son-in-law, the aforementioned Donald Bisland? In a family letter, he wrote: "The end of this story is as extraordinary as it is interesting in that before Grandpa and Harry (sic) Bentley left Baden-Baden for home they received a personal invitation from Hitler to have tea with him at Berchtesgaden. The political uncertainties of the time were such, however, that they both politely declined the invitation and drove straight home to the UK."

Now that would be a myth if anyone had ever repeated it before now.

But there was one final twist to the story of the presentation, one last piece of the evidence which would take the story further. One piece of testimony which arrived at the 11th hour of investigations and 11th hour and 59th minute of writing which, if the reader will forgive the author, we will keep to the final chapter in order to sustain the mystery...

10

TO THE VICTORS BELONG THE TREES

There was no hero's welcome home for Thirsk and Bentley on their return to England. No ticker-tape parade, no knighthood, not even a few letters after their names to mark a victory Olympic in terms of the scale of the trophy if not in actual name. There was no invitation to drinks at 10 Downing Street, the current method by which politicians attempt to bolster their popularity on the back of a sporting success.

Tom Thirsk did, however, receive a few knives and forks. And, to be fair, there were spoons as well in the canteen of cutlery that Bridlington Golf Club presented to Tom Thirsk at a dinner in the clubhouse held in his honour on November 13, 1936. The great and the good of Bridlington turned out, including the Mayor (Alderman A E Fligg) and the Sheriff of Hull (Mr J A Dew), as reported in the *Hull Daily Mail* the following day.

"Members paid tribute last night to the achievement of Mr Tom Thirsk, the international player, at Baden-Baden when he and A C Bentley won Hitler's Prize of the nations for Britain (sic)," the newspaper chronicled.

The presentation was made by club captain J D M Bissland whose only son, Donald, as chance would have, went on to marry Thirsk's only daughter, Jill, 14 years later. Bissland was suitably enthusiastic. "Even Bobby Jones in all his glory never returned a score better than Mr Thirsk over 72 holes," the captain stated.

Thirsk, he contended, would have made his name as a cricketer had he chosen cricket instead of golf. "Cricket's loss was golf's gain," he declared.

Thirsk said in his thank-you speech that he owed a debt of gratitude to Jack C Coppack, the Bridlington pro, for helping him improve his golf. The *Hull Daily Mail* concluded by informing readers that "a musical programme followed." Ah, the ubiquitous musical programme of that era.

The local council had been even quicker of the mark in officially acknowledging their local hero's success. The September 21st meeting of the General Purposes Committee of Bridlington Corporation resolved "that the congratulations of the Council be extended to Mr T J Thirsk on his success in the competition and that arrangements be made to present him with a suitable gift in commemoration of his achievement, at an early date."

The Town Clerk followed up with a letter to Thirsk informing him of the resolution and continuing: "I shall be obliged if you will please inform me as to the form you wish the presentation to take, in order that arrangements may be made for the presentation to take place."

Thirsk opted for a silver tea tray judging by the Town Clerk's follow-up letter. "Averting to my letter to you of the 5th instant," he wrote, "I have now received from Messrs Dewhirst Bros. a silver tea tray which I understand you have chosen for presentation to you by the Council for your success." All Thirsk needed now was some crockery.

"The tray will be suitably inscribed," the Town Clerk continued, "and the suggested subscription to be placed thereon is as follows: 'Presented to THOMAS JAMES THIRSK ESQUIRE by the MAYOR AND CORPORATION OF BRIDLINGTON in commemoration of his success in the GRAND GOLF PRIZE OF NATIONS competed for at Baden Baden in connection with the OLYMPIC GAMES, 1936.' "

The *Hull Daily Mail* of 10th November, 1936 provides

confirmation that the piece of silver was duly handed over. Under the headline 'Bridlington Honours Great Golfer' the article began: "One of the happiest incidents of the Mayoral banquet at the Royal Spa Hall, Bridlington, last night was the presentation on behalf of the Corporation of a handsome silver salver to Mr Tom Thirsk, in honour of his great golf victory in Germany this year, when he and A L Bentley won Hitler's 'Prize of the Nations' (sic) for Britain (sic). Mr Thirsk has brought golfing fame to Bridlington and its golf club on many occasions but his victory at Baden-Baden, on which he was congratulated by Hitler (sic), is his most notable feat."

Aside from the newspaper seemingly inventing – or at least misreporting – what would have been a historic handshake between Hitler and Thirsk, the *Hull Daily Mail*'s coverage of a local community justifiably proud of the achievement of a local sports star was anything but replicated nationwide. It was all the national press could do to report the bare result never mind any of the dramatic circumstances.

Meanwhile, despite the presence of its secretary 'Tiny' Lavarack in Germany and the fact that Messrs Thirsk and Bentley travelled in its name (though not at its expense) the English Golf Union appeared almost embarrassed at the victory. There would have been many within and without the EGU who would have wished a team had not been sent and just as many who would have wished that they had not returned with a trophy bearing the title of the German chancellor.

Whatever, the trophy now belonged to the English Golf Union. A letter arrived within a few days from Karl Henkell, the aforementioned President of the German Golf Association appointed by Hitler's sports minister, confirming that fact.

Addressed to the English Golf Union, 72 Draycott Avenue, Kenton, Middlesex, England, the letter read: "Dear Sirs, we wish to send you our heartiest congratulations on your Team's success

116

in the Grosser Golfpreis der Nationen.

"We were delighted to have Mr Bentley and Mr Thirsk with us in Baden-Baden and were greatly impressed by the quality of golf they played.

"Through their win, the Grosser Golfpreis, which was given by our Führer and Reichskanzler Adolf Hitler, becomes the property of your Union and we sincerely hope that it will further the connections of friendship and sportsmanship between English and German golfers.

"With kindest regards, we remain, yours sincerely, Karl Henkell, President."

There is no indication that the letter was penned in blood.

But the blood that was to be spilled within a few years and the attrocities carried out in the name of Nazi Germany ensured that the so-called Hitler Trophy remained an unwelcome and unloved guest of the EGU during hostilities and into the post-war period.

The trophy came with trees, just as the gold medals at the Olympic Games were presented along with potted saplings. Oak in Munich and fir in Baden-Baden. Jesse Owens, on his own, returned to America with four Hitler oaks; Great Britain as a team managed the same number, one of which remains standing at How Hill in Norfolk having been planted in his garden by victorious six metre class helmsman, Christopher Boardman.

Bentley and Thirsk returned home with one baby Black Forest fir each. Bentley planted his in a plot beside the flagstaff roughly half way between the clubhouse and the first tee at Hesketh. It stands to this day, vigorously sprawling in spite of – or perhaps because of – the treatment of the members. The Hitler Tree, as it became known, received pretty much daily watering during the war and much beyond by golfers who preferred not to confine their business to the clubhouse toilets as a statement of national pride and loathing for the German dictator. Or, as Harry Foster wrote in the *Annals of Hesketh Golf Club*, the "tree benefitted from regular applications of nitrogen enriched surplus water."

Thirsk's fir was, like Thirsk himself, pretty much adopted by the local council who decided to plant it with great ceremony in the Town Hall gardens. His son-in-law Donald Bissland's recollection was of the occasion being attended by "all the family and friends including my parents and myself, the Mayor, the Corporation, the Town Band and the public in their hundreds."

Not everyone was in favour, with the letter pages of the local newspaper offering a microcosm of mixed feelings towards the booty from the Baden-Baden venture. One correspondent raged about "rank impertinence, involving a slur and insult upon the intelligence of the Bridlington ratepayers… (a desecration of) the grounds belonging to a free-born race."

Another, taking decidedly an opposing view, described Hitler as "a man of undisputed integrity, uprightness, honesty, and loftiest ideals… a sort of modern saint." The writer went on: "The astonishing thing is that so very busy a man as Hitler should find the time to distribute things like trees to so remote a place as Bridlington." So, there we have it. Hitler, not a painter but a gardener.

The outbreak of war caused the council to change its position, and, consequently, the position of the tree. There was no ceremony this time around, as Donald Bissland was to recall. "It was not long after the war started," he later wrote in a family missive, "that the Mayor and Corporation decided it was inappropriate for there to be a tree there donated by Hitler and it was quietly taken up and replanted in the garden at Anglos on Cardigan Road (Tom Thirsk's family home), now an old people's home."

The tree was planted in ground prepared for the erection of an air raid shelter. It was subsequently removed after the house changed ownership.

As for the trophy, it presumably remained with Lavarack, the English Golf Union secretary, hidden away in a cupboard in his home so as not to open him up to accusations of being some sort of Nazi sympathiser. The EGU had no headquarters at that time, no place to display its trophies even if it wanted to. Only later did The Golfers' Club, operating as a traditional London club from premises in Whitehall Club, provide the EGU with space from which to conduct its business. In return, the EGU conferred life membership on The Golfers' Club.

It was against this background at a dinner in the club on 15th February, 1955, attended by the likes of Lord Bruce of Melbourne, the former Prime Minister of Australia and the first from his country to become captain of the R&A, that Lavarack presented what was to become known as the Hitler Trophy to The Golfers' Club. This gesture could have been by way of a thank-you or even in lieu of rent.

It could also have been, as the EGU tried and failed to maintain decades later, merely a loan for the purposes of exhibiting. No-one knows since any potentially elucidating documentary evidence disappeared in a subsequent fire which destroyed EGU minutes.

The Hitler Trophy now belonged to The Golfers' Club whose birth, various marriages and ultimate death is a story in itself.

A beautifully bound journal written in perfect Copperplate declares that in 1893 "certain gentleman interested in the game of golf" decided to form a club where they could discuss their favourite game, organize competitions and arrange matches. The first meeting took place in an imposing listed building overlooking Victoria Embankment and the Thames which today houses, inter alia, The Royal Horseguards Hotel. This magnificent building in the French Renaissance style, Whitehall Court by name, has played host to The Farmers Club and been requisitioned by the government as the HQ of MI6 during World War I. It includes among its former residents the writers HG Wells and George Bernard Shaw, Lord Kitchener and multiple Prime Minister William Gladstone.

A number of similar organisations, each with its own

accommodation, restaurant, bars etc, comprised the original occupants. The lavish amenities of The Golfers' Club comprised a dining room, smoking and reading room, card room, billiard room, bar with terrace overlooking the Embankment, bedrooms, squash courts and golf driving nets. There was a men-only policy in regard to membership though a general lounge and dining room was available for members to entertain women friends.

Clubs had become a British institution by the end of the 19th century, having evolved from coffee house meeting places of the 17th century. At first primarily political clubs like White's, their appeal broadened to encompass sport. The Royal Thames Yacht Club was instituted in 1775 followed by the MCC in 1787. The popularity of golf rose throughout the 18th century to the extent that London could boast 26 courses in the surrounding area. It was time for a London club for Londoners as well as visitors to the capital from the four home nations and indeed the entire Empire.

Among distinguished early members was the Right Honourable Arthur James Balfour, the British Prime Minister between 1902 and 1905. Balfour, a connected Scot who inherited a vast fortune at the age of 21 only to spend pretty much it all by his death at the age of 82, enjoyed a long political career to which history has not been kind. Neither his achievements nor his application towards the job in hand matched the size of his ego.

You can gauge his attitude to life in the following quotation. "Give me my books, my golf clubs and my leisure," he said during his Premiership, "and I would ask for nothing more. My ideal in life is to read a lot, write a little, play plenty of golf and have nothing to worry about."

As attractive as that might sound to many, it does not seem the best philosophy for a Prime Minister burdened with affairs of State. Balfour, like Lord Bruce, was a PM who became an R&A captain. What "little" Balfour wrote – though, in truth, he penned a great deal – included a book on golf. Apparently a gifted pianist as well as a qualified philosopher, he continued to play golf – and tennis – into his 79th year when illness and infirmity intervened.

The Oxford and Cambridge Golfing Society was formed in Whitehall Court in 1898. The English Golf Union met there, as did both the British Senior Golfers' Society and the Golf Society of Great Britain; the Ladies Golf Union gathered there to select Curtis Cup teams. The Lady Golfers' Club, founded in 1912 and amalgamated with The Golfers' Club itself half a century later, also occupied rooms in Whitehall Court.

The Golfers' Club became part of elegant London with a membership exceeding 700 in 1908. And it accumulated its own elegant golfing memorabilia, including some exquisite custom-made mahogany straight back chairs, featuring crossed, hand-carved golf clubs on the backs with a hand-carved golf ball between the club heads at the base. These were owned by the Ladies Golf Union and now sit in St Andrews.

Many a famous amateur golfer visited for meetings or perhaps a drink and a meal. Cheap overnight accommodation proved a strong draw. The burgeoning world of television was represented with the likes of Eamonn Andrews and Cliff Mitchelmore paying their membership fees. The later years of life at Whitehall Court saw the club stage a series of successful luncheons to which prominent people were invited. Prime Minister Jim Callaghan turned up for one.

The bubble burst in the late 60s, however, when following a change of ownership of Whitehall Court, The Golfers' Club was given notice to quit. Nothing was ever the same again as the club was forced to find a new home. Then another, then another, then another.

It initially landed softly enough in 1969 in rooms at the back of the historic Devonshire Club at 50 St James Street, directly opposite White's. The Devonshire Club operated for more than

100 years on that same site, from its formation in 1874 to its closure due to financial problems in 1976. Bringing in The Golfers' Club as well as a Masonic group on the top floor was intended to be part of the solution to money difficulties. To no avail. The Devonshire Club had initially flourished but it never really succeeded in emerging from the shadow of those two great Liberal institutions, the Reform Club and the National Liberal Club.

Fifty St James Street, for which the Russians paid £75 million several years ago, had been the address of Crockford's, a notorious illegal gambling den in the first half of the 18th century. William Crockford, the son of a fish and chip shop owner, accumulated a huge fortune essentially from fleecing the aristocracy attracted to the establishment by its raffish reputation. Gastronomy proved just as important as gambling in the success of the venture, though. The Duke of Wellington was a regular without ever making a bet. The great Duke was attracted, like so many, by the sensational free suppers dispensed by celebrated (and fabulously paid) French chef Eustache Ude. Ude's previous employers had been, in chronological order, Napolean's mother, the Earl of Sefton and the Duke of York.

The Womens Golfers' Museum was also allocated a room fronting on to Arlington Street. Things did not work out and pretty soon the golfers were being urged to move on the prospect of a sale. So, in 1973 The Golfers' Club packed up their trophies, including a certain amber inlaid German novelty, and shuffled off to 10 Old Burlington Street. It might just have been 10 Rillington Place since the new base almost did for the club.

The key deficiency, as the head of the club, Gordon O. Davies (GOD to the members), conceded in hindsight, was the lack of accommodation. The fact that special terms had been arranged for rooms at nearby hotels failed to satisfy the members.

"The value of accommodation had not been realised until

none was available for members at the new premises," Davies admitted. "Membership dropped drastically and something had to be done and done quickly."

That something was yet another move. In 1975 The Golfers' Club affiliated with the Sesame, Pioneer and Lyceum Club at 49 Grosvener Street, an amalgamation of three originally women's establishments. Dame Edith Sitwell, the English poet and critic, lived in the club in the years prior to her death in 1964. Crucially, there were 44 rooms available in an atmosphere of old world charm. Arrangements were also made for members to use the Sloane Club in Lower Sloane Street.

"Again disaster struck," Davies reported in his short history of the club. "The Sesame Club gave The Golfers' Club notice to quit. To the committee this was a devastating blow and for a time it looked that in spite of surviving two world wars and all the vicissitudes associated with and created by them the Club was doomed.

"Then at the last moment the club was saved by a very keen golfer and important industrialist who took over the responsibilities of the club," Gordon Davies added.

Enter a wee Glasgow businessman by the name of Leonard Sculthorp.

11

THE TYPEWRITER KING OF GLASGOW

Leonard Ernest Sculthorp is a driven individual with a lifetime of business success from Scotland to Florida who, well into his 80s, is still writing letters to the Prime Minister about pension matters and still on the lookout for opportunities to make money.

He sits at a large paper-strewn mahogany desk in the bay window of his Pollockshields pile on the outskirts of his native Glasgow, telephone, mobile, computer and fax machine to hand, pausing only in his wheeling and dealing to lunch on Cup-a-Soup and accompanying ham and tomato sandwich. On white bread, of course. This is the west of Scotland.

There was a time in the late 1970s when Sculthorp was viewed as a potential saviour of The Golfers' Club. Gordon Davies, the long serving secretary and president of the London club, thought so when entrusting the future of his beloved organisation to a chartered accountant and industrialist with a proven midas touch. Davies' faith proved misplaced with the club barely stuttering along before ceasing to operate in 1996.

"It was one of the things I failed in," Sculthorp told the author. "Perhaps the only one I really failed in. I was never able to make anything of the club. I told Gordon Davies I would. If you fail, you fail. No excuses. I should have done better. I had hoped my son and daughter would have done something better."

It was not for the lack of trying.

Sculthorp was born into the family firm of office equipment

suppliers. Grandpa Sculthorp, Ernest by name, a Londoner, had travelled to Glasgow in 1900 to take part in the Great Scotland Exhibition, scheduled to take place the following year. He never went home. Not exactly, but when the exhibition was over he remained in Glasgow to go into business on his own.

He was doing well until the outbreak of the First World War when low-priced imports from the Continent flooded the market. The years after the war proved difficult. Ernest was eventually joined by his son, William, Leonard's father, in 1925 and sufficient capital was raised to create Sculthorps Ltd. With William as managing director the firm moved into premises at the corner of West Nile Street and Bath Street. There they remained and grew, both in terms of space and scope, the typewriter kings of Glasgow who expanded and modernised with the advent of adding machines and all manner of office equipment.

Spacious showrooms and stockrooms were opened; specialist departments were created; demonstration rooms were added as more property was bought. A staff of four in 1918 had grown to 130 in 1963. The small showroom in Buchanan Street had mushroomed into 14 different departments. Sculthorps opened in Edinburgh and stationed a full-time representative in Dundee.

By the early 1960s, Leonard Sculthorp, a qualified chartered accountant, had joined the board and assumed responsibility for the running of various departments.

"I remember my grandfather well," Sculthorp said. "The old man was quite a well known character. He wore a fresh rose on his lapel every morning in life and sported a big moustache. When a wee boy I would get sixpence if I kissed him. It was not really worth it. You could set your clock by him as he paraded down to the pub every morning at 10.50 with the horses going up the street pulling beer barrels."

William Sculthorp had fought in World War I. He was a police reservist during World War II and further did his bit for the country by repairing army typewriters. "It was my father who branched out into office furniture and built up the company," Leonard explained.

Young Sculthorp was educated at the High School of Glasgow, alma mater for a whole host of distinguished Scots, including a pair of Prime Ministers in Campbell Bannerman and Bonar Law. His training as a chartered accountant was carried out at the Institute of Accountants in Glasgow. Sculthorp was always destined to join the family firm but first there was the small matter of National Service.

"I wanted to go into the navy with my pals. Their surnames were Anderson and Brown, A and B at the beginning of the alphabet. They got in, no problem. I was an S. By the time it came round to me there were no navy places left. I wondered how I could use my knowledge of sailing and enjoy life for two years.

"I heard about the Royal Army Service Corps. They were in charge of the harbour in Hong Kong. I could get a commission, be put in command of a torpedo boat and be surrounded by half naked women. As it happened, my commission came through and, according to my script, I was posted to Hong Kong. But it was just an illusion.

"Just before I was due to travel, the Suez Crisis erupted and there was an order from the War Office for the first available accountant to report to 5 Training Battalion at Aldershot. That was me. So much for Hong Kong and swim-suited girls! I went into the army in 1954, came out in 1956 and never left Aldershot. But that was where I met and married my lovely wife, Ena.'

Sculthorp had assumed full control of the company in the years immediately prior to his father's death in 1966. He set about turning the originally small Glasgow family firm into a Scottish, indeed British, and even international powerhouse. By the time he was finished, he had multiplied by 500 times a turnover of £200,000 into one of £100 million in a company – later called

Office International Group, UK – employing upwards of 2000 people. Job done.

"I was going at such a rate that we needed capital. So we joined British & Commonwealth and came under the umbrella of the holding company, Caledonia Investments. My best man was a shipping and forwarding agent in a company that looked after British & Commonwealth in Glasgow. He introduced me to Jim Thomson, a Scottish chartered accountant and financial director with B&C. He was interested in what we were doing at a time when shipping was beginning to die."

These were very big players indeed. British & Commonwealth grew out of Clan Line Steamers, founded in 1878 by the legendary Sir Charles Cayzer and developed into the world's biggest cargo ship fleet. The purchase of the iconic Union-Castle Line paved the way for the creation of the British & Commonwealth Shipping Company. Meanwhile, Caledonia Investments has morphed into the self-managed investment trust ODF today, premium listed on the London Stock Exchange, with assets of £1.6 billion.

The secretive Cayzer family still own almost 50% of the share capital.

"I built the business town by town," Sculthorp said. "I was involved in about 60 takeovers. I became President of the Association of Office Machines and Equipment Federation and that helped me in growing the business."

Although the headquarters remained in Glasgow, Sculthorp was doing most of his business from London, where he had acquired a flat to stay in during the week. The weekend was for the family which he would pack into his car and drive over the Rest And Be Thankful road to a rented house in Argyll, an association which lasts to today. The papers which clutter his desk are mostly concerned with the ownership and operation of his estate in Argyll.

While in London he met and became friends with Gordon

Davies. Both loved their golf. Sculthorp had played rugby at school, a typical speedy wee Scottish wing threequarter. But he was also a golfer, first at Cambuslang then at Strathaven near to where the boy and his grandmother were evacuated during the war. It was back to Cambuslang before joining his father at Cathkin Braes. Ultimately, Sculthorp would become a member of the Glasgow Club at the parkland course at Killermont, the gravitating point for any self respecting city businessman.

Sculthorp and Davies discovered a mutual interest in reviving the fortunes of the ailing Golfers' Club. Davies, a honorary member of the Isle of Man Golf Club, had battled in vain to turn round a club suffering from the natural demise of London gentlemen institutions and the attendant handicap of frequently being required to up sticks. The membership had fallen to just 300, though nowhere near that number used the facilities with any regularity.

In Sculthorp, Davies identified a keen golfer, a sharp business brain and a trained accountant who appeared to have both the financial acumen and imagination required to sort out the debt and reinvent the club.

"Gordon Davies was getting on, well into his 70s," Sculthorp recalled. "He did not have anyone to take over. He became interested in me because of my accounting background. There was a lot of that in managing a club. I had this idea of building the club up at an international level. I was keen to reach out to the likes of South Africa and America."

The quid pro quo for Sculthorp was to use golf – and therefore the club – as a vehicle to expand his own business. He made no bones about it. "I saw it as a commercial opportunity. I was thinking of golf as something I could use for my business. We were going after financial directors and the like of big companies and most of them were golfers. I saw them as members of The Golfers' Club. I saw a way of spending my advertising budget in a unique fashion, not just on advertising. At the same time we could grow something of great interest."

Entirely coincidentally, The Golfers' Club were at that stage using facilities at the Sloane Club. The Sloane Club happened to be owned by British & Commonwealth who, in turn, were in the process of becoming the majority shareholder in Sculthorp's business. Sculthorp himself had nothing to do with putting The Golfers' Club and the Sloane Club in touch with each other. He was more surprised than anyone to discover the link.

The Golfers' Club became a proprietary club in 1978 when it was bought by Sculthorp under the banner of O.I. Golf Promotions Ltd. "I didn't pay anything for it as such. I took over debts and we had to invest in it. We went to a few sales people and got ideas of how to build it up. It never actually happened. I was too busy and the people I got to do it did not find a way of bringing everything together to make it work."

Among the few assets acquired by Sculthorp were the club's trophies and honours boards. The latter pieces of memorabilia remain rather unceremoniously stuffed behind a sofa in his Glasgow home.

The Hitler Trophy itself stood in its case anything but proudly on a bar counter in the Sloane Club, largely ignored and only occasionally remarked upon by inquisitive visitors. Arnold Bentley was only a few streets away, as it happened, oblivious to the location of the trophy he had helped secure for his country. Nor did he have any idea that this curiosity was to become the focal point in the next chapter in the history of The Golfers' Club. The London club was moving to St Andrews.

More precisely, it was being relocated to a farm several miles from the 'auld grey toon'. The plan was to turn an ancient hilltop watering and resting place for monks on their pilgrimage to St Andrews into much the same for golfing pilgrims. It would be known as Dron Court.

Property had always represented another side to the restless mind of Leonard Sculthorp. When he was not trying to buy an island on the west coast of Scotland or building holiday homes in the Mull of Galloway, he could be found battling with the council for permission to do something similar at Loch Ness. If it was a pastime, as he insisted, something different and away from his main business, then he took it seriously enough to become the chairman of the Association of Self Caterers in Scotland. Self catering was then a new way for people to be able to afford better holiday accommodation and/or add to their assets.

Prior to embarking on the Dron Court development, Sculthorp purchased a flat on the corner site of the old Links Hotel at the side of the Old Course 18th green and the most photographed clubhouse in golf. He used this first floor flat, offering an unmatched view of golf history in the making, to entertain clients. As the supplier of typewriters and office equipment to the Open Championship, tickets were not a problem.

On May 18, 1984, The Golfers' Club became The Golfers Club (St Andrews Ltd). And Sculthorp set about converting the farm out-buildings into 14 holiday homes. A clubroom was built at the centre of the complex with the Hitler Trophy its centrepiece.

"It never crossed my mind that anyone might be upset about the Hitler element of the trophy," Sculthorp insisted. "I just thought it was an interesting story. The war was long over. I was not of the age that got so upset about what had happened, Maybe it's hard to believe, but it did not affect me at all in relation to the piece of silverware. It was just part of what I was trying to do."

It was around this time that Sculthorp was sucked into a messy and highly public reorganisation at British & Commonwealth. A new broom was sweeping clean and the tenacious little Scotsman was one of those swept away in the process. Sculthorp felt that at 54 he was at his peak. So, he launched himself full time into his property and building interests which included the development at Dron Court. His son, Brian, and daughter, Elaine, were enlisted and given The Golfers Club as one of their responsibilities.

A 10-point strategy for the new club, devised in 1988, outlined plans way beyond anything previously achieved or imagined in the 95 years of the club's existence. Reading it gives an impression of part vaulting ambition and part pure fantasy.

■ To find the recipe which will create membership at several levels by meeting the aspirations of each group of members and giving them the feeling of comfort and value for money.

■ To encourage golfers to travel to the United Kingdom and help them enjoy their golf and feel comfortable while visiting courses in this country.

■ To create a club atmosphere for members in several major conurbations in the United Kingdom. This will require a partner or partners.

■ To find a recipe whereby golf clubs will become members of The Golfers Club to create business for themselves through the use of their courses at quiet times by our members who could pay full green fees.

■ To arrange twinning of clubs in this country having a long tradition with newer clubs which have developed across the world. This could, if successful, create major tourist movements of club parties to the United Kingdom.

■ To create a mail order business by offering specialist golfing and other luxury goods manufactured in St Andrews or Scotland to members and perhaps at a slightly higher price to the members of golf clubs who are in turn members of The Golfers Club. Golfing books and videos would also be made available but perhaps through specialist existing distributors such as W. H. Smith.

■ To create a stock of golfing mementoes, memorabilia and antiques and offer items to top level of membership on a regular basis.

■ To create a small team of people who could find items of

special interest to members, including property in the United Kingdom. This service would be available on a fee basis.

■ To create a Golfers Club Tournament in St Andrews for its centenary year in 1993 and continue, if successful, on an annual basis thereafter.

None of those ambitions, even the less lofty, was realised. It was, as stated, not for the lack of trying. The Sculthorps hired a marketing consultant, Philip Gregory Associates, only to be told what many would think was the bleeding obvious – namely that The Golfers Club required a permanent home in St Andrews, not a holiday park several miles away. You could imagine the reaction of a group of wealthy Americans, for example, who had planned a trip-of-a-lifetime in St Andrews only to discover themselves isolated inland and very much in the hinterland.

Approaches were made by the family to first the Scores Hotel then the refurbished Old Course Hotel with a view to forging a relationship that would provide a St Andrews base for the Golfers Club and accommodation for the members. They came to naught.

Jack Nicklaus was contacted offering him the role of patron of the club. He declined, politely of course.

It seemed that no-one shared Sculthorp's vision of a marketing concept based on golf. On reflection, Sculthorp thinks the problem was one of timing. "I think that had the internet been in existence then we might have been huge. I had an idea of golfers booking tee times around the country through The Golfers Club. You would be a member of a golf club but also a member of The Golfers Club. We would have special Christmas sales, wives as members, all sorts of things. If you can build up a club and it is not too expensive people can be snared for life. Give them a wee pat on the back every now and then, something prestige wise. You get a bankers order for something like 20 quid and you have got it for life."

But Sculthorp could not heave The Golfers Club even to first base. Although the Glaswegian did not enjoy failure and had not tasted it all that often, he knew it was time to move on. Dron Court was sold in 1990, as were the houses he owned in the Mull of Galloway.

"Dron Court did not really happen," he conceded with obvious regret. "As I was semi-retired, I went to Florida."

Typically, though, Sculthorp did not head to the Sunshine State to improve his tan and his handicap, though he did both. In fact, he took most of his money out of Scotland and invested in Florida. His new company, Floridron Ltd (you see what he did there), proceeded to build more than 400 houses in six new developments in Indian River County on the Treasure Coast, starting with the aptly named St Andrews Village. Plans to use the company to take Scottish golfers to Florida in the British winter and Florida golfers to Scotland in our summer were deferred, such was the preoccupation with real estate.

Everything went swimmingly, so to speak, through the 90s and into the new Millennium, excepting the extensive damage to the Sculthorp's own Flordia house by Hurricanes Frances and Jeanne, a double whammy of storms in September 2004.

A bit of structural rearrangement did not amount to a hill of beans compared to the carnage of the 2007 financial crisis. "Everything fell apart," Sculthorp recalled. "We had to sell everything. We were left with three houses which we rented out when people stopped buying. Brian still has his interests in the Bahamas and Elaine is still heavily involved in the travel industry. I also sold my house in Florida when my wife, Ena, became ill and returned to Scotland."

Still, there was no sign of retirement. Today, in his 85th year and almost swamped by the clutter on his desk, Sculthorp is renting out a couple of luxury houses on his Dunmore Estate in Argyll and trying to sell plots. The sales pitch is never far from his lips. "Accounting wise, building a new house is much more economic.

Why pay the government? You pay for a plot and everything else is tax free and VAT free. The thing to do is buy plots."

The Golfers Club survived the sale of Dron Court but not the ravages of time. The hard-hearted businessman that is Leonard Sculthorp eventually closed down the club in 1996, a decision he took not lightly and with sadness but also with his eyes wide open. The inevitability of the historic institution's fate had been apparent for years.

The peripatetic Hitler Trophy never travelled to Florida. When Dron Court was sold in 1990 it headed for Glasgow and Sculthorp's home on the outskirts of the city. And there it remained, packed away in its wooden box, untouched, unloved, ignored and forgotten about.

For 14 years, other than the very occasional reference in a golf publication, nothing was heard of the brass and amber enigma. Until one day in March, 2004, Sculthorp was alerted to a story in *The Scotsman* newspaper. A whodunit, or rather whereisit, was penned under the byline of Mark Lamport-Stokes which referred to a book on the Olympic Games written by George Jeanneau of the French Golf Federation.

"Since then," Lamport-Stokes wrote, referring to the 1936 tournament at Baden-Baden, "there has been no further update to this intriguing story. The trophy, one of the most unusual prizes in golfing history, remains missing, possibly stolen. If it still exists, it is possibly gathering dust in an attic or a cupboard. Should it resurface, it would certainly make a unique, if not widely popular, addition to golf's varied assortment of silverware."

Hey, wait a minute, Sculthorp told the *Daily Telegraph* Scottish Correspondent, Auslan Cramb, in so many words. "Speaking from the poolside (don't they always in newspaper reports) of his second home in Florida," the *Daily Telegraph* reported, "Sculthorp explained that the trophy was owned by a limited company of which he and members of his family were the sole shareholders.

"I have always been amused by stories about the Hitler Cup (sic) going missing," he was quoted as saying. "It has been safe in my house in Pollockshields since the 1990s."

In September, 2003, Sculthorp and his wife had journeyed south to a Carlisle hotel to show the trophy to Peter Thirsk, Tom's son. Thirsk, who had never concealed his anger at the English Golf Union allowing the trophy to slip from its grasp, had never previously seen the salver that his father had done so much to win.

And following the newspaper articles in 2004 two men travelled to Glasgow to meet with Sculthorp. They were Bobby Bentley, Arnold's son, and Derek Holden, the President of Hesketh Golf Club. The visitors saw the trophy 'sitting' on the sofa before joining Mr and Mrs Sculthorp for lunch at Haggs Castle Golf Club where Mrs Sculthorp was a member.

Sculthorp and Holden were never to meet again but both men were heavily involved in what followed over the subsequent years until the Hitler Trophy found a final resting place.

12

CAN WE HAVE OUR TROPHY BACK?

Derek Holden insists that his interest in the Baden-Baden golf event of 1936 and the subsequent mystery surrounding the Hitler Trophy never became an obsession. He prefers to call it a passion.

But Holden wrote two booklets on the subject – a 20-page 2005 publication entitled *Adolf, Arnold & Tommy* backed up by a 24-page 2012 revision with the same title – and organised a fund with the aim of buying the trophy at auction. He spent countless hours on the projects.

Holden is now an active 81, still fit enough to play two rounds a week at his beloved Hesketh Golf Club. He has been a member of the Southport club for 65 years, having joined as a 16-year-old in 1950. He was honoured with Life Membership in 1989 and appointed Honorary Life President in 2006.

Born in Southport and educated at King George V School, Holden spent his working life in the retail trade, initially following his father into the photographic equipment business and eventually owning the Apple Centre in Preston. The early link up with Apple turned out to be a prescient move. "It was a tough time which suddenly got better," he recalled.

Holden first met Arnold Bentley in the 1950s. The friendship began to grow in 1967 when it was not uncommon for Holden, the club's youngest ever captain, and Bentley, pretty much the club's best player, to play together on the occasions of the latter's return from London.

"It was not a close friendship at that stage," Holden explained. "But, despite being 20 years younger than Arnold, a strong friendship grew between us. We played many rounds together before an injury to Arnold's heel forced him to give up the game. And two or three times a week we would be in the same company who enjoyed conversation at the bar."

Bentley proposed Holden for membership of the Royal and Ancient Club at St Andrews which came through in 1982. In the last competitive round they played together at Hesketh, Arnold, playing off a handicap of six, won both the gross and net prizes beating a number of the club's most talented youngsters in the process.

Bentley's modesty and reticence were so substantial that it was not until 1986 that Holden heard in greater detail the story of the Baden-Baden tournament and the Hitler Trophy. The spur for Bentley opening up on the subject was a centenary book (The Hesketh Golf Club 1885-1985, written by Keith C Hick and curiously published in 1986) which included a newspaper cutting from Scotland's biggest selling newspaper, *The Sunday Post*, headlined 'SO HITLER WENT OFF IN THE HUFF.'

"To Arnold, it was something from the distant past," Holden said. "As far as he was concerned, the trophy had disappeared. But he always became pretty animated when there was a report with inaccuracies. The *Sunday Post* article enraged him. He scored things out and wrote corrections all over the page of his own personal copy. "

Bentley, in fact, was moved to write the following correction and clarification which is included in Holden's booklet:

"I do not know from where the writer obtained his information, nor by his term 'Exhibition Sport' – it was in fact an International Tournament for a prize presented by Adolf Hitler, Führer and Reichskanzler, designed to coincide with the Olympic Games, which were taking place in Germany in 1936.

"The International Trophy was NOT Foursomes Knock Out as stated, but was STROKEPLAY over Four Rounds to be played by each player, all Eight Rounds to count.

"TOMMY Thirsk – NOT TONY – I would have thought that his initials T.J. Would have suggested that his name was not Tony (Anthony).

"In the afternoon WE did not have a record round, Tommy Thirsk did – he had a 65 – I took 75...

"England won the Trophy by FOUR STROKES over 144 holes - I would not have considered that to have been 'Won by HANDS DOWN', as suggested by the writer."

You can almost see the steam rising from his words.

Holden's interest buds had been activated. But it was not until the death of Arnold Bentley in 1998 that Holden began to think about "setting the record straight". Holden recalled: "I knew that Arnold got really irritated by inaccurate reporting of the event and I thought it would be a fitting memorial to him if someone could print the true story."

Hence the *Myth, Mystery and Fact* sub-titles to both his booklets.

Holden found willing supporters, helpers and fellow research allies in two sons who, independently of each other, were annoyed that England - and specifically the English Golf Union - had given the Hitler Trophy away. They wanted it back, preferably to their own family and certainly to a suitable location in England.

As Holden wrote: "Although living vastly different lives, at opposite sides of the country, and divided by the Pennines, the two sons share a common belief that if the EGU had been installed in their magnificent Woodhall Spa headquarters in 1936, it is highly likely that Hitler's trophy would have been given a permanent display site. They find it difficult to understand what possessed the administrators of English golf to almost flippantly dispose of a national trophy that had been fought for and won by their fathers on the links at Baden-Baden."

These two men were Robert Bentley, a former flying instructor, and Peter Thirsk who was in charge the family milling business previously run by his father. Sadly, Thirsk died in 2012.

Robert Bentley had always wanted to be a pilot; his father wanted him to get a "proper job". So Bob, as he is known by most of his friends, embarked on the dentistry profession. Not for long. His urge to fly prevailed. He had become a flying instructor and just obtained a commercial pilot licence when one late March day in 1978 his world changed.

On March 28, Piper Cherokee G-AWBD took off from Woodvale Airfield, near Formby on Merseyside, on a dual-control cross country training flight to Carlisle. Three men were on board, Bentley, the flying instructor, and two young students, including one only 17 years old. Bentley, himself, was a pretty tender 25.

Although the weather was clearly deteriorating, Carlisle and Blackpool were still 'flying', i.e. open, when the Piper Cherokee headed North West. Pretty soon, with storm clouds ahead, Bentley informed Carlisle of his intention to turn round and head back to Woodvale.

"I turned round and flew into a wall of thick cloud and turbulence," Bentley recalled. "The plane became instantly covered in snow and we experienced airframe icing, the pilot's worst enemy. This is where the air flow is broken. I told my students this was no longer a flying lesson, this was a case of just getting home."

Bentley found himself in the nightmare position of trying in vain to keep his nose up while in actual fact the plane was descending with the weight of the ice.

"I saw a whiteness which for a split second I was unable to distinguish as cloud or snow. I was heading straight for it. Then I spotted a smooth snow-covered slope going upwards. I thought – uphill landing, that will soften the blow."

The covering proved skimpy and not much of a cushioner.

The plane landed on huge rocks under a dusting rather than blanket of snow – one of which tore through the floor of the cockpit on Bentley's side – in a gorge just below Scafell Pike. The two trainee pilots, though trapped in wreckage like Bentley, were pretty much uninjured. Not so Bentley.

For 30 hours, including one overnight, the three men lay in freezing cold temperatures. Bentley was unconscious for most of the time. It was not until almost dusk on the second day that a passing group of hiking schoolchildren from Watford Grammar spotted the wreckage and raised the alarm.

Bentley remembers much of the details of the crash with the protection of black humour. "I was thinking: what the hell are these kids doing out walking in this weather? But they saved my life. I would not have lasted another night. As it was, the medics who airlifted me to Whitehaven thought they heard my final death rattle during the flight.

"I was very, very lucky to be alive. If we had been flying in the opposite direction with the strong winds at our back I would have been strawberry jam."

As it was, Bentley spent a year in the spinal injury unit at Southport, having had his spine broken in three places. Fortunately, the spinal chord did not snap. Only after the spinal people did their work could he be handed over to the orthopaedic specialists. Frostbite pretty much did for both Bentley's feet.

"I lost the toes at first, then the balls of my feet and finally my arches. My feet were eventually amputated right back to the heels. There was a stage when it looked as if both my legs would be amputated. I think my young wife left me because I was going to be in a wheelchair the rest of my life."

Bentley's feet were operated on 25 times as part of a surgical litany which is continuing to this day, 37 years on. At time of writing, Bentley was preparing for a second shoulder replacement.

Bentley flew again but he found it too difficult and eventually stopped. The accident also did for his golf which somehow made it more important for him to appreciate his father's success on the course. That, in turn, led to him taking a great interest in Derek Holden's efforts.

Holden and Bentley travelled together to Glasgow late in 2004 following the publication of stories identifying the location of the 'missing' trophy.

"We went up to Scotland to see Sculthorp," Bentley recalled. "He had it lying there on a settee in his home. He had acquired it with a job lot and when the Golfers' Club left London he took it to Scotland. He and his wife took us to a nearby golf club for lunch. We had a general natter, really, and took some photographs. I think he told me his company had their own private plane."

In fact, Holden and Bentley had inquired about buying the Hitler Trophy. Sculthorp said it was not for sale. At that stage, Sculthorp still looked at the amber panels and saw golden eggs from a golden goose.

"The trophy was on the sofa, alright," Sculthorp confirmed. "No, it wasn't for sale at that time. We discussed letting them take it down South for a club dinner or something. I was amenable to that providing they insured it for £125,000. They baulked at that."

Holden still sounds incredulous when looking back to that meeting. "He wanted us to insure it for £125,000!" The exclamation mark remains after more than a decade.

Holden and Bentley had been beaten to the punch, as it were, by Peter Thirsk who had arranged to meet Len Sculthorp – and trophy – in a Carlisle Hotel the previous September. He was thrilled to be photographed with the trophy.

"It was a proud moment to hold the trophy my father won," Thirsk later told the *Daily Telegraph*. "Seeing the Hitler Trophy for the first time meant a great deal to me. Father also received two silver vases for being the overall winner, which are still in the family."

Peter Thirsk was one of twins born to Tom Thirsk while he was rushing back from playing for England in the Home Internationals in Northern Ireland in 1933. Peter eventually took over the family flour-milling firm from his father. His retirement, ending 47 years in the business, saw him increase the time he spent researching his father's golfing achievements.

"My father died in 1979," Thirsk wrote in an article on the subject, "and I regret not having had the opportunity to speak to him at length about this trophy, which, with his partner Arnold Bentley, he won for this country. Being a modest man, he never spoke about his golfing successes."

He had written to Arnold Bentley almost 20 years earlier requesting assistance in getting the trophy back. The reply from Bentley demonstrated his support but not what one would describe as a burning desire to rectify the matter. There is, too, a flavour of modesty in the reading between the lines.

Bentley wrote: "It (the Trophy) should have been kept by the EGU to whom it belonged. I can only think that when Major Lavarack, the then secretary of the EGU, retired, nobody claimed the trophy back from the Golfers Club. I agree entirely that the trophy should not be held in Scotland and should be in England either at the EGU or as you suggest in an English Golf Club.

"I, of course, knew your father well, having played in the England international team with him in 1936/37/38 and on many other occasions. But I am now 75 years of age. I really do not want to get involved in trying to get the trophy to Hesketh – they already have a photo of it – my memento prize salver and a gold medal which you no doubt have from your father.

"I could, therefore, as you request, give my blessing to you to try and obtain the trophy. I would suggest for Bridlington Golf Club, the club named on the trophy as the course from which your father played – but I do thank you sincerely for letting me know your thoughts."

Thirsk was determined not to let the issue lie. A study of the correspondence between Thirsk and the English Golf Union over that period shows a man seeking explanations and failing to receive them.

A letter dated 30th October, 2003 from Paul Baxter, chief executive/secretary of the EGU, to Thirsk states: "I suspect the Executive Committee would have made the decision to present the Trophy (to the Golfers' Club); however, the Union was run on totally different lines in the 1930s and it may have been a decision taken by the Council."

Holden, too, was pursuing the matter. On 25th August, 2004, Baxter wrote to Holden: "The Council Minutes of 1935 and 1936 do record the invitation to an International golf tournament being organised in conjunction with the Olympics of 1936, our participation and success. I am not sure how and when the trophy got into the hands of the Golfers' Club or what happened to it thereafter. We may have some records of the decision to loan/give it to the Golfers' Club although this might take some finding."

That same year, in an article for *Through The Green*, Thirsk concluded: "Two questions remain as to why the EGU, who must have known of the demise of the Golfers' Club, made no effort to regain their trophy. And why was it that the 1936 salver was selected for the original donation? No answers to these questions are apparent."

There remain no definitive answers. But it is reasonable to assume that, given the horror of the events that unfolded, the EGU were embarrassed at taking part in the tournament, winning it and then receiving a trophy bearing the titles of Adolf Hitler. It took the best part of 20 years but eventually the EGU got rid of it.

There came a time when Len Sculthorp was happy enough to get rid of it. But not at that stage. Not when there was still a chance to make commercial use of it; not when people were beginning to take an interest in the trophy. Holden and Bentley had not travelled to Glasgow for a holiday. Thirsk had made no bones about the fact he wanted the trophy back in England.

Writing to Derek Holden in January, 2005, Peter Thirsk made reference to Len (Sculthorp) as a "very pleasant and highly successful businessman" and to him and his wife Ena being "a charming couple". But he added: "I did find him very defensive when talking to him about how he acquired the trophy. He is no predator but perhaps he feels a little guilty about how he got his hands on such a memorable trophy. He has long had an interest in things golfing and when his company bought the premises of London Golfers Club (sic), I think it must have been the icing on the cake for so much memorabilia to fall into his hands. I certainly bear him no grudge and am only upset that an English sporting trophy was not looked after by its recipients."

The recipients were, of course, the English Golf Union. There is evidence that an overture was made to Len Sculthorp with a view to retrieving the trophy. Keith Wright wrote to the Scot at the Golfers' Club at St Andrews shortly after taking over as secretary of the EGU in the 1980s. Under the heading, The Hitler Trophy, the letter read: "I understand from my investigations that the above trophy is in your club at the present time. As I am sure you are aware, the trophy is an international one, won in 1936 by two players representing England, and I would very much like to talk to you about this particular trophy. I should be most grateful if you could contact me by phone or drop me a line indicating where I can contact you so we may discuss the matter."

To put it bluntly Sculthorp thought the letter a bit of a cheek. So, he replied with what the baseball fraternity would call a curve ball and cricketers a googly.

"Dear Mr Wright, we are well along the path of reorganisation of the Club from premises in St Andrews and during our full examination of the history of the Club through the minute books

I came across the following entry: 'Tuesday, 4th February, 1958 – Committee Meeting. The chairman read a letter from the English Golf Union… in which it was pointed out that the Golfers' Club under EGU rules was an honorary member and in accord with Rule VIII was entitled to nominate two members from the Club to serve on the EGU Council annually. Two members were nominated on the EGU Council for 1958.'

"Would you be good enough to confirm that the Golfers' Club continues to be an honorary member and to be entitled to nominate two members to the council?"

The discussion that Keith Wright sought never happened. Not that the EGU could have afforded to buy back the trophy. The Hitler Trophy continued to reside in Scotland, initially at the Golfers' Club new headquarters outside St Andrews and then in Len Sculthorp's Glasgow home.

"I was showing it to the occasional visitor from down south," Sculthorp recalled. "The Hesketh people and Iain McKinnon Douglas from Ganton where Tom Thirsk played a lot of his golf."

There was, too, a visit from a distinguished German who took time out of a Scottish holiday to view the trophy. Dietrich Quanz is an eminent Olympic historian who founded the German Golf Archive in Cologne and has written extensively about how Hitler used the Olympic Games for propaganda purposes. Nowadays not in the best of health, he still delights at the day he held the trophy and seems almost as thrilled at learning Sculthorp's son was a mounted policeman.

It was during this period that it was suggested to Sculthorp that the International Olympic Committee might want to purchase the trophy for the Olympic Museum in Lausanne. An approach was made but the IOC were not interested.

It was now July, 2008 and the Hitler Trophy was on the move again. To a museum, though not the Olympic Museum.

13

UP FOR AUCTION

In July 2008, Len Sculthorp packed the Hitler Trophy into its substantial wooden box to be dispatched to the British Golf Museum in St Andrews. The Museum, located on the opposite side of the road from The R&A Clubhouse, had opened in 1990 as a central focal point for golfing memorabilia from the middle ages to the present day.

It was reopened after a lengthy closure for extensive rebuilding and refurbishment on its 25th birthday in 2015. A modern website, showing that golf can occasionally move with the times, boasts a collection of more than 17,000 objects including such highlights as Tom Morris Junior's Open Championship Medal, some Bobby Jones 'flicker' books, Henry Cotton's MBE and the shoes Seve Ballesteros wore when winning the Open at St Andrews in 1984.

Both Sculthorp and his son, Brian, had contacted the Museum to offer the trophy as a loan. Although the trophy no-one wanted had become the trophy many coveted, it seemed that no-one was prepared to match its Scottish owner's estimation of its value. It was not making money. It was sitting in a Glasgow house in need of some love and attention. The Museum was only too delighted to accept the trophy into its safe keeping. A 12-month gratis loan was agreed to be renewed on a year-to-year basis.

"It was an interesting piece and for obvious reasons also a difficult piece," curator Kevin Knox said. "We were delighted to give it a home."

The Museum chose not to include the trophy in its Olympic section, preferring to place it alongside other exhibits from the inter-war period. The trophy was regarded as separate from its Olympic exhibits among which were a photograph of Jedburgh's Walter Rutherford, the runner-up in Paris 1900, and an interesting silver medal made for the abandoned 1908 Olympic golf event.

Instead, the Hitler Trophy found itself in the company of a letter from the German Golf Association to Harry Bentley, Arnold's older brother, giving him permission to take the German Amateur Trophy, which he had just won, out of the country. The date was August 17, 1939, just a fortnight prior to the outbreak of World War II.

And there, with the Firth of Forth almost lapping the doorstep, the trophy remained for two renewals of the loan. But not a third. It left the museum in December, 2011 and returned to Glasgow, having spent three and a half years among shelves groaning with golfing history.

"I decided I no longer wanted or needed all this," Sculthorp said. "I decided that because we had spent a lot of time and money on the Golfers' Club without success, we needed to try to recoup some of that. My daughter and son, who had been directors of the club during its period as a limited company, had also devoted a great deal of effort on this project. When you add up the money spent on sales people and consultants it ran into thousands of pounds. We had to recover what we spent."

The plan was to auction the trophy, to sell it to the highest bidder, regardless of who and regardless of where.

In fact, the Hitler Trophy might well have been auctioned off 36 years earlier. During the depths of the financial crisis, with the Golfers' Club bleeding with debt, Gordon Davies reluctantly approached Sotheby's in London with a view to putting it up for sale. It never happened.

It was going to happen second time around. Brian Sculthorp

contacted Kevin McGimpsey, the golf specialist at Bonhams, and preparations were made for the trophy to be included in the Sporting and Golfing Memorabilia Sale to be held in Chester on May 29, 2012.

Derek Holden had not forgotten about the trophy won by his dear friend Arnold Bentley. But he had heard nothing about it since his visit to Glasgow until one day over seven years later a fellow Hesketh member mentioned that he had seen an article in a golf magazine about the forthcoming auction. Several members passed on the same information.

"I was interested, of course," Holden recalled. "But I remembered the £125,000 insurance figure required by Sculthorp and I thought the price would be prohibitive. However, the subsequent Bonham's catalogue valuation was a reasonable and manageable £10,000 to £20,000. The possibility of Hesketh acquiring the trophy became no longer unthinkable."

Two members each offered a four-figure sum to launch a fund. Other members matched that. Pretty soon a fully-fledged fund-raising operation had swung into action. A series of posters were exhibited in the Hesketh clubhouse outlining the history of the Trophy as far as it was known and informing members of any developments.

Financial pledges were often accompanied by messages of support which touched Holden enough for him to keep a record of them. Some examples: "I've always been intrigued by the Bentley brothers and proud that I am a member of a club with such rich history. I think it's important that the club attempts to secure this piece of history."

"How odd it has been to receive your email as I sit in my hotel bedroom in Berlin! I would be pleased to offer £200 to the bidding pot. It has to be right that we must not ignore the chance of retrieving part of Hesketh's historic fabric."

"Just returned from a week in Scotland where the golf clubs

have long histories and some fantastic memorabilia on display. But there is nothing to match the Hitler Trophy and it should have pride of place at Hesketh."

Not every member shared those views or were prepared to share their savings. Not every member agreed with the project and by no means every member contributed.

"Like every golf club, there were disagreements," Holden said. "Some thought we were wasting money on it; one of two were vehemently anti-German and did not want to have anything to do with it; one Jewish lady in particular was very upset and resigned from the club. The reluctance on the part of some underscored how difficult it was to separate the salver from the dark period in which the tournament was born. But the committee agreed this was something worth doing."

Holden wrote in the revised edition of his booklet: "The strategy for persuading the membership to get behind the Club's bid was to contact them regularly, and as the auction date got closer, the campaign intensified. It was important to keep everyone informed, to maintain momentum, but not exert undue pressure."

At that stage, Ganton, the golf club most associated with Tom Thirsk, was also interested in acquiring the trophy. Ganton is a historic club with royal connections whose fine course, a regular in the top 100 in the world, has hosted the three most established team events in the world, the Ryder Cup, the Walker Cup and the Curtis Cup, as well as a plethora of championships.

The Prince of Wales agreed to be patron of the club in 1895. A frequent visitor to Tranby Croft, near Hull, he would play golf at Ganton when in the area. The locals might well have felt let down that having ascended to the throne in 1901 King Edward VII did not feel disposed to bestow the accolade of 'Royal' to the club to join the likes of Royal Lytham, Royal Birkdale and Royal St Georges. Ganton did enjoy a second royal connection via Prince Arthur of Connaught, a grandson of Queen Victoria. He was club president from 1913 to 1931.

Uniquely, Ganton can boast two club professionals, the great Harry Vardon and Ted Ray, both Jersey men as it happened, who won both the Open Championship and the US Open. When Tony Jacklin won the latter at Hazeltine in 1970 he became only the third Briton to win the Open titles on either side of the Atlantic.

Ganton has also produced many a fine amateur player. Tom Thirsk's bosom buddy and golfing partner was Bill Stout who, as if his name were not intimidating enough, was known as the 'long-hitting Bridlington dentist'. One presumes he drilled the ball into the distance. Stout was reputed to have driven Ganton's 18th green at a time when the hole measured 300 yards and the equipment predicated against such length from the tee.

Stout was also known to have recorded a 2 at all but one of the holes at Ganton for an eclectic score of 37 during a distinguished career which included victory in the English Amateur at Royal Lytham in 1928. Twice a Walker Cup player and an England teammate of Thirsk, the dentist became the captain, the president and an honorary life member in his years at Ganton. Stout, whose range of talents extended to music, also played league cricket. He was larger than life, a genuine all-rounder and a true local hero.

Thirsk, too, achieved the Ganton triumvirate of captain, president and honorary life member. And as if to cement his reputation as a team player, he won 22 of his 40 matches for England between 1929 and 1946, halving eight and losing only 10. Among the trophies on display in the clubhouse are the two silver cups Thirsk received at Baden-Baden and a silver candlestick known as The Thirsk Trophy which the player himself presented to Ganton in memory of his daughter Jill Bissland, tragically killed in a car accident in America.

It seemed that Ganton had as many credentials as Hesketh to house the Hitler Trophy. Perhaps even more more. Had not their man Thirsk, rather than Bentley, made by far the greater contribution towards victory with his score 22 strokes lower than his teammate? There are some who would have viewed it that way, though probably not Thirsk, the ultimate team man, as mentioned previously.

Piers Shepherd, a military medal expert and private collector, was Ganton captain that year. His view on hearing about the auction was: "Let's see if we can get some money together." Shepherd is a member of the Shepherd Construction family who grew to become a huge company from modest beginnings, not least because of their development of the ubiquitous Portakabin. He has a reputation of being a tough, uncompromising individual who does not suffer fools gladly.

Ian Douglas, who is well known throughout the North in golfing and rugby circles, was involved in the fund-raising as club archivist. "There was a certain resistance, as one might imagine," Douglas recalled. "Some, frankly, thought it a load of bollocks. But others were keen. It seemed obvious that it would do neither Hesketh nor ourselves any good to bid against each other. There was talk about us putting in a joint bid and perhaps playing each other in a match in an Olympic year with the winner earning custody of the trophy in the intervening period."

In fact, the two clubs did play each other twice, not in Olympic years, before the match fell into abeyance. But the trophy was never at stake.

It was full steam ahead at Hesketh. An undertaking was given neither to identify donors nor to reveal the amounts given. Such was the sensitivity surrounding something so obviously associated with Nazi Germany. Although contributions were received from young and old, long-established and new members, the broadest burden was carried by a few.

"The Club's Captains raised 60 per cent of the total and there is no question the project would not have got off the ground but for them," Holden said.

The Lancashire and Yorkshire clubs kept in touch and reported on progress. Lawyers were consulted to investigate any problems associated with a possible shared bid. The Royal & Ancient Club was asked if it was interested. No, came the reply with the diplomatic comment that it would be appropriate for the two clubs to share the trophy. Bridlington, Thirsk's first club and the club out of which he was entered in Germany, declared they did not wish to become involved.

Eventually, there was a meeting arranged between Ganton and Hesketh. This was High Noon, though the agreed meeting place was not a small western town in New Mexico but, less romantically perhaps, a motorway service station on the M62 near Huddersfield. Holden and the club treasurer represented Hesketh; Ganton was served by Shepherd and Douglas. It proved not the most harmonious of occasions.

"It was clear from the outset that Hesketh had raised a lot more money than us, that we were not able or prepared to bid for the Trophy ourselves and that Hesketh wanted to go it alone," Douglas remembered.

"Piers was a bit annoyed. He said that if it meant so much to them then let Hesketh get on with it. Acquiring the trophy clearly meant more to them than it did to us. Never mind that it was our guy who won it. So that was that.

"It was a Godsend, really because it turned out that we could use the money raised, plus some more, to buy a painting we had been after for years. The Harry Rountree watercolour of Ganton's 18th green came up for sale from a private collector in America shortly afterwards and it now hangs in our lounge." A photograph of the Hitler Trophy, in contrast, is tucked away rather unceremoniously on a wall above lockers in the visitors' changing room.

Holden confirmed that he attended the meeting for the purpose of telling Ganton that Hesketh intended to make its own bid for the trophy. "It was done reluctantly but it had become clear

152

that, providing Bonham's valuation was in the right area, we had raised enough money to acquire sole ownership. It had also become apparent that the people prepared to pledge money thought that the club should set its sights on becoming outright owners. No donor made that a stipulation, however."

Hesketh had negotiated a deal with the local council for a contingency back-up which would be available if the funding fell just short of the hammer price. That was intended to be repaid by an extension of the appeal. Enthusiasm reached such a level in the days and weeks before the auction that one member offered to fund the entire project with an interest-free loan, up to £35,000.

There was a final message on the eve of the auction from Bob Bentley. "I really hope that Hesketh does become the home of the Trophy, where I feel it now belongs," he emailed. "A private owner would probably hide it away. Tom and Dad would not deserve that to happen again. All the best and good luck with the bidding."

14

AZALEAS DON'T BLOOM IN SUMMER

Everyone who was anyone in global golf administration had gathered one warm October evening in 1992 in the southern comfort of the Augusta National clubhouse for mint juleps, dinner and a discussion intended to influence the future of the sport.

Among those present were Billy Payne, the workaholic Georgian who had conceived and masterminded bringing the 1996 Olympic Games to Atlanta, Deane Beman, the long-standing PGA Tour commissioner widely regarded as the man who turned golf into a billion dollar business, Michael Bonallack, respected secretary of the Royal and Ancient, and Jackson T Stephens, the billionaire chairman of the Augusta club.

Stephens, who spoke with a buttery Southern drawl, had graduated from the same 1946 class at the US Naval Academy in Annapolis, Maryland, as President Jimmy Carter. Stephens went on to create Stephens Inc., the largest off-Wall Street investment banking firm in the country. Among his many philanthropic gestures – most of which were never publicised – was a five million dollar donation for the launch of the First Tee Programme, the highly successful international junior golf development organisation.

Stephens, a close friend of Bobby Jones, was the chairman at Augusta National from 1991 to 1998 during which time he introduced the now famous – and sometimes cringe-making – Green Jacket presentation ceremony in the Butler Cabin.

There is a story about Stephens which says much about his

wealth and even more about his character. It concerns a mouthy new Augusta member from Detroit who liked to bet almost as much as he loved to let people know his financial worth. The pair met for a round with the newcomer suggesting stakes in multiples of 100 dollars.

"My, that's impressive," Stephens is reputed to have said, "but we keep our betting to 10 dollars here. It makes the game more personable."

The man from Detroit continued to urge extra wagers as the round progressed with Stephens choosing neither to accept nor comment. Golf over – we do not know the outcome – they repaired to the members' card room for some gin rummy, the preferred game at Augusta National. Stephens suggested "a penny a point", American parlance for a cent.

"You've gotta be kiddin' me," Mr Michigan said. "We play for a dollar a point."

Stephens had had enough. He asked the irritant to add up all his holdings - his stock, his real estate, his homes, his car and his cash etc, the whole nine yards as they say – and put a figure on what he was worth. Somewhat taken aback, the man eventually came up with an estimate of between 15 and 20 million dollars.

"Right," said Stephens, "I'll cut you for it!"

We are talking wind and sails and removal of, not to mention red face at night.

It would not have been known at the time that Billy Payne would take over as Augusta chairman in 2006. He was not even a member in 1993. Membership was granted in 1997, the year after the Olympic Games.

William Porter Payne was born in Athens, Georgia, the son of the Georgia Football captain, Porter Otis Payne. He inherited his father's determination and, considerably less welcoming, a genetic problem with his heart. Payne suffered his first heart attack at the age of 26, underwent a first bypass operation at 34 and required a second bypass in 1993. Nothing, though, diminished his work ethic, unless one counts the single concession for health reasons of putting back the start of his working day from 4.30am to 5.30am.

Payne had a dream. He wanted the Olympic Games to be staged in Atlanta. The first person he told was his wife, Martha. She was reported to have responded by telling him he was crazy. Payne ran the idea up the flag pole of Andrew Young, the former US Ambassador to the United Nations and the Atlanta mayor. "This guy's a nut," was his apparent reaction. No matter, he agreed to open doors, as it were, for the lunatic.

Payne was a salesman, a trained property lawyer who could sell anything. Even the idea of Atlanta staging the Olympics when on the 100th anniversary of the start of the Modern Olympic Games it was really supposed to return to Athens. And, glory be, with irony self evident, the man from Athens, Georgia, who wore a "Hi, I'm Billy" badge on his lapel, ran a campaign which did for Athens, Greece.

Payne had another dream. He wanted golf to be included in 'his' Games and he wanted the tournament to be staged at Augusta National, some 150 miles down the road from Atlanta. Just about the first person he told of his idea was Juan Antonio Samaranch, the president of the International Olympic Committee, whose reaction was favourable. Samaranch's son, Juanito, was a single figure handicap player and in, for example, the great Seve Ballesteros, the old man had several prominent Spaniards nipping his head on the subject.

Michael Bonallack had been the most successful British amateur golfer of his generation when beginning his 16-year stretch as secretary of the R&A. He had won five Amateur Championship titles between 1961 and 1970 and twice, in 1968 and 1971, finished leading amateur in the Open Championship. His curious crouching putting style in no way diminished a lethal short game backed up by a cool temperament and steely resolve. Bonallack became no less respected as an administrator to the extent that few, if any, would have argued with his deserving knighthood in 1998.

"I remember we all flew to Augusta at short notice," Bonallack recalled. "We had dinner and the talking began. Payne spoke about his idea of including golf in the Atlanta Olympics with the request that it be held at Augusta. I have to say I expected Jack Stephens to say it was impossible. The course is always closed between May and October when, basically, everything is dug up and relaid for the following year's Masters.

"Surprisingly, Stephens said that would be fine. He said Augusta would replace the rye grass summer covering with Bermuda to cope with the hot sun.

"Deane Beman was very doubtful about the timing. He said he would be losing one of his lucrative tournaments that week. Stephens asked if it was a question of money and, if it was, not to concern himself. Stephens said that Augusta would pick up the tab and compensate the PGA Tour for any loss of earnings. That seemed to satisfy Beman. We were asked to report back to our committees. We played golf the next day and that was that."

The R&A had been when not hostile then at best luke warm to golf being an Olympic sport throughout the 20th century. Even into the 1990s there was a lingering feeling that any sport in which the pinnacle was other than an Olympic gold medal should not become an Olympic event. The same argument against tennis – which was eventually overcome – applied to the golf. Bonallack carried back to St Andrews a note for Neil Roach, the then chairman of a championship committee that had been consistently opposed to golf joining the Olympic movement.

But the R&A decided to join the United States Golf Association and Payne's Atlanta Olympic Committee in making an official presentation to the Programme Commission of the IOC in Lausanne. That committee was chaired by Philippe Chatrier, the Frenchman who had led tennis into the Olympic movement in

1988. He also happened to be married to Claudine Cros, the former French women's golf champion. In the circumstances he was certainly not going to dismiss the proposition out of hand.

"The proposal was for 72 holes strokeplay with no qualification process and the countries nominating their players," Bonallack recalled. "We all had to say something. The committee reconvened the next morning and said they were going to recommend to the IOC that golf be admitted. It was extraordinary. We were all very excited. It seemed as if we had achieved this out of the blue."

And that was how close golf came to being welcomed back into the Olympic family 20 years earlier than it eventually was.

That the plan never saw the light of day was down to a miscalculation on the part of Billy Payne. He knew he had the support of Augusta National and the various golfing associations around the world; he knew he had backing from the Programme Commission of the IOC; he knew that the President of the IOC, no less, was in favour of golf joining the movement. But he did not count on the level of hostility from black activists and equality campaigners horrified that the all-male, white preserve of Augusta National might stage an Olympic event. Nor were some leading figures in the Atlanta business community exactly thrilled at the prospect of golf taking place a three-hour drive from a city which could boast its own splendid golf courses. Peach Tree, for example, Bobby Jones's other alma mater.

Atlanta City Council passed a resolution in opposition to the plan because of alleged discrimination at Augusta National. The mayor, Maynard Jackson, wrote to the IOC pointing out the qualities of golf courses in Atlanta and the immediate neighbouring area. Payne was verbally attacked over and over again and drew such anger from some quarters that pickets parked themselves outside his home. He attracted fire from from former Olympic rowing bronze medallist Anita DeFrantz who had become the first woman and first African American to represent the United States on the IOC. DeFrantz apparently fumed at both the plan and the fact that she had not been consulted by Payne.

There was also some negativity from US television. Golf is an unwieldy and expensive sport to cover because of the acreage involved, the number of cameras required and the uncertainty about where and when the story of the day would materialise.

Samaranch did not need all this controversy. He fashioned a hasty about turn, telling an Italian newspaper early in 1993 that golf had little chance of being approved. The following day Payne, realising the Bermuda grass had been taken from under his feet, released a statement announcing that the proposal would be withdrawn. The home of the Masters would not be a home for the Olympics.

Just how close Augusta came to hosting golf at the Atlanta Olympics was revealed in the Programme Commission Report to the 101st IOC Session held in Monaco three years earlier. The report stated: "At the suggestion of ACOG (the Atlanta Committee for the Olympic Games, i.e. Billy Payne), the sub-commission received a delegation from the World Amateur Golf Council who wished to include golf in the programme for 1996. The majority of the commission approved the idea. But ACOG, for its own reasons, finally withdrew the project." Maybe just as well. The azaleas don't bloom in the summer.

"It was probably not the right time," Bonallack reflected. "It was probably too soon. There was still a lot of at best ambivalence within the Royal and Ancient, the USGA and the PGA Tour. The issue had probably more opponents than supporters among those organisations. Things have changed. There are far more countries now involved in golf and the television coverage is now large enough."

Payne did not take that view. He was to remark during the Atlanta Olympics, "It's clear the biggest thing missing here is golf at Augusta. I'm sorry about that. It is my biggest personal disappointment."

The post World War II years had brought precious little mention of golf on the Olympic front. The IOC had declared as far back as 1921 that for a sport to be considered for inclusion it had to played in at least 40 countries and it had to be run by a single international governing body. Golf failed on both counts, especially the latter. The R&A and the USGA shared governance of the amateur game and of the rules while the various Professional Golfers Associations around the world looked after their own.

There was the odd intervention in that period. In 1959 the mouthful that was Count Pierre Marie Xavier Raphael Antoine Melchior de Polignac wrote a letter to John D Ames, the president of the USGA, suggesting that his organisation pursue the case of golf returning to the Olympics. Prince Pierre of Monaco, as he was mercifully better known, the father of Prince Rainier III (and, therefore, father in law of Grace Kelly), was the president of the Monaco Olympic Committee and a member of the IOC.

Ames, a newspaper publisher and investment banker who as a Lieutenant Colonel in the war held the position of deputy military governor of Rome, replied briefly and to the point. He said that the World Team Championship perfectly served the interests of amateur golf.

A motion was put forward at the World Amateur Golf Council general assembly in 1964 that an attempt should be made to reintroduce golf into the Olympic Games. It was unanimously rejected for reasons of a crowded tournament calendar and a belief that some of the bidding and hosting cities would not be able to offer the competitors an adequate test of golf.

That aside, the subject remained largely dormant until 1976 when *Golf Magazine*, an American publication, called for renewed debate. Lord Killanin, the Irish President of the IOC, was unambiguous in the negativity of his response. He told the magazine in an interview that the IOC had not received a single official request to reinstate golf into the Olympic programme. He also pointed out that such a request would have to come from an international federation and golf did not have one. It still had two masters, he insisted, the USGA and the R&A.

As if that were not enough of a damp towel, he pretty much extinguished any embers of hope by adding: "If golfers ever want to be part of the Games they will have to be prepared for a long, hard fight and they have to take the initiative. Never is a term I do not like to use but I am not optimistic on the entry of golf to the Games in the near future." The noble Lord would be proved right on that one.

The 80s saw the Western European countries, in particular Spain and France, scatter the seeds of Olympic thoughts only for them to fall on the stoney-faced officials at the R&A and USGA. Again and again the European Golf Association would make representations to the World Amateur Golf Council only for their efforts to be ignored. Luis Figueras-Dotti Cabot assumed the presidency of the Spanish Golf Federation with a stated prime intention of squeezing golf into the 1992 Barcelona Olympics, at least as a demonstration sport.

Claude-Roger Cartier, the president of the French Federation and the secretary general of the French Olympic Committee, told a press conference at St Nom-La-Breteche in late autumn 1989 that the World Golf Association, which he headed, would be going all out for demonstration status in '92 ahead of full admission in '96. A gap would be left in the schedule for professionals and amateurs. "If players do not have the Olympic spirit, they don't come. I think we have a 50 per cent chance of getting back into the Olympics come Atlanta.'

Within a couple of months, however, the IOC announced the abolition of demonstration sports. Golf was snookered.

The formidable Emma Villacieros, whom former European

Tour chief executive Ken Schofield likes to describe fondly as the Margaret Thatcher of golf, assumed control in Spain and made it her life's work to reintroduce her sport into the Games. It did not take her whole life but it took up her entire presidency from 1988 to 2008, plus another year of expectant retirement.

George O'Grady, who had taken over from Schofield, was in a confident mood when just a couple of months ahead of the eventual decision to readmit golf he said of Villacieros during a ceremony making her an Honorary Life President of the European Tour: "Throughout her presidency (of the Spanish Federation) her lifelong ambition was to see golf admitted by the Olympic movement. It speaks volumes for her powers of persuasion if golf's application to be included in 2016 is successful."

Tough, persistent and indefatigable, Villacieros was in her own sphere every bit as fierce as Thatcher. She was not for turning. Not as far as the Olympics were concerned. In Cartier, she had her Norman Tebbit, Cecil Parkinson and Keith Joseph rolled up into one. Together the pair bombarded the conservative administrative voices in golf with the message that only Olympic golf could provide funding and profile to grow the game in Europe and around the world. And when the Berlin Wall came down that applied as much to Eastern Europe as the comparatively more established countries like Spain, France, Germany and Sweden.

Schofield, the Perthshire banker and St Johnstone football supporter turned European golf supremo, remembers well the period when those in charge of both professional and amateur golf needed a lot of persuading about golf rejoining the Olympic movement.

"I took over in 1975," he said. "I don't think it was in anyone's thoughts for about the first 10 years. There was never any talk at that time about the Olympics. Then our regular meetings with the European Federations to discuss dates occasioned many a fierce debate about golf in the Olympics. I remember one heated discussion in Copenhagen, ironically the location in 2009 when the IOC voted golf back into the Games.

"The principal movers were the Spanish, the French and the Scandanavians. Their message was constant: golf in the Olympics would give them a higher standing with their sports authorities and open the way for government funding to build the game in their countries. Emma and Claude were always most insistent. This was a Western European thing. There was no golf in Eastern Europe, the communists did not allow it. And the Americans never saw any need for it.

"It was always thought to be something for amateurs, that if golf returned it would be strictly for amateurs. That changed definitively in 1997 when Juan Antonio Samaranch, the IOC president, was our guest at the Ryder Cup at Valderrama. Emma thought it a great opportunity to press her case with her fellow countryman in front of all the top officials. Samaranch spelled it out clearly: if golf entertained any hope of joining the Olympics it would need to involve the best players in the world. He went further. He said that if we could guarantee participation of the best players he would get us in. Unfortunately, he did not stay around long enough."

All of which begs the tantalising thought that had Samaranch applied for re-election in 2001 golf just might have made it into the London Olympics in 2012 with Wentworth a likely venue.

As it was, Samaranch handed over the reins to Jacques Rogge, the former Belgian Olympic sailor. Golf was to discover that the goalposts had been moved or, more appropriately given Rogge's sporting past as a sailor, the wind had changed direction.

"It turned out that the change in IOC presidency was not good for golf," Schofield recalled. "Tim Finchem, the PGA Tour commission attended the Salt Lake City Winter Olympics as a guest of ABC, the American television network. Finchem was introduced to Rogge who said categorically there would be no special

163

treatment for golf. As far as he was concerned – and he was boss – golf was going to have to take its chance along with the rest of the sports hoping to get into the Olympic schedule. The message was that golf would be required to campaign hard to gather enough votes."

Finchem had a few years earlier visited Wentworth during a PGA Championship and had a planned sit-down with Emma Villacieros and Claude-Roger Cartier. The idea was for Finchem and his reluctant PGA Tour to see the passion and hear the arguments at first hand rather than just be presented with a soulless paper case for golf to become an Olympic sport.

"It was not an overnight conversion but I think Tim returned to the States with the realisation that golf was a world game and a large part of the world could and should benefit from being in the Olympic Games," Schofield said. "We at the European Tour had been keen and very supportive for quite a while. We formed the opinion pretty quickly that the Federations on the Continent of Europe had a point. We valued our relationships with these Federations who enabled our tour to grow stronger by helping us get the tournament dates we wanted. Golf had clearly not developed as quickly in Europe as it had in Great Britain and Ireland. These were sensible people making the sensible argument that a place in the Olympics would attract the support of their governments and help grow the game."

But the professional game in America still needed convincing. With many of the top US players against – or, more subtly, not in favour of – inclusion, the PGA Tour withheld their public support. Finchem may have left Wentworth more intrigued by the case for the Olympics but he was not ready to declare his support. Not yet.

When lobbying began again for golf's inclusion, the PGA Tour remained silent on the matter. "It's certainly an interesting concept and we are not against participating," a Tour spokesman said at the time, "we are just not actively involved in anything to do with the Olympics right now."

Amid concerns of an Olympic gold medal comparing unfavourably beside a Masters Green Jacket, the Claret Jug and the Ryder Cup, Tiger Woods said in an Associated Press interview: "I don't think it would be a big priority in our game, just because we have four major championships with equal significance every single year."

The result was that golf made what Peter Dawson, the immediate past chief executive of the R&A, described as a "half-baked" attempt to be elected onto the Olympic programme at the IOC session in Singapore in 2005.

"We still did not have an organisation structure that was easy for IOC to interface with and we did not have the backing of the professional bodies," Dawson explained. "Golf was not speaking with one voice at the time and we were not as advanced with anti-doping policies as we needed to be."

If there were any lingering arrogance among golf officials about golf's right to be seated at the top Olympic table then it was blown to smithereens by the outcome in Singapore.

Of the five sports put forward by the Programme Commission for admission - golf, karate, squash, rugby sevens and something called roller sports – golf embarrassingly received the fewest votes. To be beaten by squash and rugby sevens, both of whom had been campaigning for some time, was fair enough but to lose out to people chopping bricks in half and pedestrian precinct pests deserved to ring alarm bells in the global golf community. Apart from the deficiencies highlighted above by Dawson, The Programme Commission had warned in their advance report that "there is no certainty the top professionals would take part."

The programme evaluation, conducted by secret ballot, asked IOC members to state 'yay' or 'nay' to the existing 28 sports under review. By that unsophisticated process baseball and softball were

165

voted out. Squash and karate would have been voted in had either of the sports achieved the requisite two thirds majority. Both fell short with the result that London staged 26 sports instead of the previous 28.

There was another result. Golf determined to get its act together and do everything in its power to secure Olympic inclusion next time around.

15

BACK IN THE OLYMPIC FOLD

Peter Dawson and his International Golf Federation colleagues were confident that they had thought of everything when they presented to the International Olympic Committee the considerable documentation associated with the sport's bid to be included in the 2016 Olympic Games. This was in 2009, still several months before 121st IOC Session in Copenhagen where the final decision would be taken.

"I remember sitting at the meeting thinking we were ready to go," Dawson recalled. 'Jack Nicklaus, Colin Montgomerie and Annika Sorenstam were with us. I thought we had all the answers to all the questions we were likely to be asked. And, pretty much right off, Frankie Fredericks (the former Namibian sprinter) asked: "Where are the caddies going to stay?"

"We were not expecting that. Just for a moment or two we looked at each other with blank faces. Then Ty Votaw said brilliantly: "It will be like the grooms in the equestrian events." It was a great answer. Everything went really well after that."

The bid team really ought to have been clued up for that one. But it illustrates the exhaustive details that a sports federation has to prepare when trying to gain admission to the Olympics.

Dawson and Votaw had become the twin powers of the bidding process, the former as chairman of the IGF and the latter as executive director of the newly founded IGF Olympic Committee. Dawson, at his best a one handicap amateur golfer, had followed Sir Michael Bonallack, the previous secretary, to become the first chief executive of the R&A at a time when the priority for the position had changed from golf administrator to business-man. Dawson, a Cambridge University engineering graduate, had been the head of sales and marketing in Europe, Asia and the Far East for Grove Engineering, the largest manufacturers of hydraulic cranes in the world, as he liked to say.

Votaw represented American interests. The son of a carpenter and a lawyer by profession, he is a graduate of both Ohio University and the University of North Carolina. He had been the Commissioner of the Ladies Professional Golf Association between 1999 and 2005 prior to marrying, not without controversy due to potential accusations of favouritism, the European Solheim Cup player Sophie Gustafson from Sweden. The couple were later divorced. Votaw made the switch from women's golf to men's golf administration on joining the PGA Tour in 2006, first in international affairs and then as the chief marketing officer.

PGA Tour head man Finchem - albeit the last of the major figures to do so - came out in support of golf being an Olympic sport in April 2008. Writing in a blog on the PGA Tour website, the Commissioner stated: "I see two very positive developments coming from including golf as an Olympic sport. One would be a significant boost to the popularity and perception of golf all around the world. While golf is a developed sport in the US, Canada, the UK, Ireland, Japan and some other countries, it is only a minor sport in many countries.

"The other is that it would further help bring the world of golf together to work on this major initiative. Adding golf to the Olympics would provide another dimension to our competitive landscape. I do not believe Olympic golf would have any effect on the stature or prestige of these other events but rather would provide another, complementary opportunity for our players to compete and demonstrate their skills on the global stage."

Dawson, David Fay, head of the United States Golf Association, Finchem, George O'Grady, the top man at the European Tour, and Caroline Bivens of the LPGA met with Jacques Rogge the following month. It was a whole lot better meeting than the discussion Finchem had with the IOC president at Salt Lake City six years earlier.

"It was important that the IOC saw the game was united, which I think they were impressed with," Finchem said at the time.

Within a matter of weeks, that unity was trumpeted at a showpiece press conference during the Open Championship at Royal Birkdale when the IGF Olympic Committee was launched. This was the moment at which professional and amateur golf began to speak with the clear one voice that had been absent at the humiliating vote of 2005. The PGA Tour effectively loaned out Votaw for the 16 months up to the IOC session in Copenhagen to lead an Olympic Committee comprising representatives of the rulemakers and all the professional major championships, both men and women. Fifty years had passed and initials had changed several times since the World Amateur Golf Council had been formed in 1958. This was no overnight revolution.

Until then golf had lacked the single international federation which, a prerequisite for all Olympic sports, administer the whole sport, runs a world championship and interfaces with the IOC.

"I think it is fair to say that when I took over from Michael (Bonallack) there were different views about the Olympics within the R&A," Dawson recalled. "This was still the period when the larger organisations felt there was a sufficiently crowded competitive landscape. The people who ran the major championships wanted to protect the supremacy of their events. The women's game were quick to give their support for Olympic inclusion but the men's game in the United States was slow.

"But there were other persistent voices from smaller nations, often in Europe. They argued again and again that becoming an

Olympic sport would mean much more exposure for the game, much greater recognition from their governments and increased national funding.

"There came a point where it became quite difficult to be on the top committee and not recognise the vast majority wanted golf in the Olympics. As part of our responsibility to the affiliated unions we had to investigate it. And let's face it, golf's popularity was under some pressure. The recurring message became that Olympic golf was the biggest 'grow-the-game' opportunity available. So, we decided to go for it."

But would the leading professional players go for it? Like the tennis players before them, there was an initial reluctance borne out of a heavy playing schedule, the pre-eminence of the four grand slam events and the vast amount of money available on a weekly basis. One quotation that did the rounds, attributed to an unnamed member of the Tiger Woods entourage, declared somewhat sourly: "It's just another week when he plays and doesn't get paid for it." This, mind you, from a representative of just about the highest earning sportsman in the world who could afford more than anyone else to play for his country rather than for bucks. It sounded very much like Mr 25% speaking rather than Mr Woods.

Woods, though, was initially against the idea, as was the majority of professionals. Those who were in favour among the established stars of the era, Ernie Els and Nick Faldo to name but two, thought the Olympics more suitable for amateur golfers or perhaps pros at an under-25 level.

Greg Norman, meanwhile, became almost evangelical in his support after being persuaded by the late, great and much missed Seve Ballesteros. Probably because of the enthusiastic noises coming from Spain and the fact that Samaranch was a fellow countryman (with a golf-mad son), Ballesteros was one of the first of the big names to speak up for golf as an Olympic sport.

Norman, speaking after the Spaniard's premature death, was

to pay tribute to his friend's forward thinking. "I remember when it started," he recalled. "It was in a practice round in 1984 at Wentworth. We were getting ready for the World Match Play Championship and Seve mentioned the Olympics. I was kind of taken aback. I hadn't thought about it. I didn't know much about the concept."

This was anything but idle chatter. Seve wanted Norman's support. Typically, Norman gave it some thought, asked around, did a bit of studying and eventually came on board. "I give Seve as much credit as anyone," the Australian added.

Norman even managed to find a message in the Olympics from his own hugely successful but – strictly in terms of the large number of major championship near misses – slightly disappointing career. "You know what I love about the Olympics? If you win a bronze medal, you are a hero. If you finish third in a golf tournament you are a choker. That's what we should all take away from the Olympics."

(Norman, as it happened, made an unsuccessful bid to design the new Olympic course in Rio de Janiero in tandem with former Mexican world number 1, Lorena Ochoa. As did the pairing of Jack Nicklaus and Annika Sorenstam.)

Speaking of that 'stellar double act', as the Americans would call it, arguably the greatest man and woman players in the history of the game, the IGF Olympic Committee could scarcely have done better in naming Nicklaus and Sorenstam their global ambassadors in December 2008.

"I can't think of any other sport that belongs in the Olympics as much as golf," Sorenstam said. "It's a global game and some of the values we see in golf are hard to find in any other sport." Talk about immediately earning your fee.

"For me it's 'Hey, you are not done yet old man. You can still contribute to the game,' " Nicklaus declared.

Dawson and Votaw visited Beijing for the 2008 Olympic

Games, primarily to press flesh and introduce both themselves and the merits of golf to IOC members but also to begin to understand the scale of the requirements. "We had never seen anything like it. The sheer size of the media and television operation, for example, was extraordinary. The Olympic village as well," Dawson said.

There followed in 2009 presentations to the IOC Programme Commission in Lausanne, to the IOC executive board in August and finally to the 121st session of the IOC in Copenhagen in October. Dawson and Co had taken along to the Programme Commission the 1904 Olympic Golf Trophy which had been provided for the occasion by the Royal Canadian Golf Association. "I don't think some of the members knew that golf had been in the Olympics before," Dawson commented.

Things went well, if agonisingly so, at the Executive Board meeting, which was required to make a recommendation to the full session. Rugby sevens secured one of the two available recommendations with a majority of nine votes in the second round. Golf, which received only one vote in the first round, gained the necessary majority only in the sixth round. Jacques Rogge suggested, according to *The Official History of the Olympic Games and the IOC*, "that in addition to youth appeal, universality and good governance, the decisive factor had been the geographically wide availability of iconic competitors and an ethic that stresses fair play."

There was still the final hurdle to clear, still a chance for something to go wrong, still the admittedly unlikely possibility that the full membership of the IOC would take a different view from the Executive Board. Dawson, Votaw and four professional golfers comprised the presentation team, all of whom were scheduled to speak.

No problem for Irishman Padraig Harrington who kissed the blarney stone on the way to winning two Open Championships

(2007 and 2008) and one USPGA Championship title, also in 2008. Except for one thing. Harrington was not comfortable using a prompter or reading a speech. And he would not have been permitted to ad lib because his words had to be translated into many languages in advance.

What did he do?

"I learned it off by heart," Harrington explained.

It was a measure of the man and of his passion for golf becoming an Olympic sport. Harrington had been an early and energetic advocate. "It is a big deal in Ireland to be an Olympian," he said. "Some golfers say we now have four majors (and that's enough). But the four majors were not the four majors 70 years ago. You never know, in 50 years time maybe the Olympics will be the No 1 major. It has to start somewhere."

Harrington, very much the experienced major winner, was joined by Matteo Manassero, then just 16 having earlier that year become the youngest winner of the Amateur Championship. The Italian spoke articulately in English but could have made the same speech in four other languages. His was widely acknowledged as an impressive performance and not just for someone of such tender years.

Michelle Wie was a comparatively ancient 19 at the time when she told the delegates: "When you represent your country, this takes you to a whole new place, the highest honour for any athlete." She was joined by LPGA major winner Suzann Petterson from Norway to complete a deliberately diverse quartet of age and gender. There was also an important contribution from Tiger Woods whose final words in a slick video were described by Dawson as "very powerful."

The eve of the big day had brought humour and panic in equal measure for the golf delegation, as Dawson recalled. "We had hired a consultant with experience of IOC procedure. We were all ready to go when they guy said, 'I think we should do the first bit of this in French.' Now, Ty was supposed to open proceedings and Ty did not speak a word of French.

"You should have seen his face. You could not see him for dust as he ran down the corridor. Maybe I exaggerate. Anyway, it was decided that I should take over that section from Ty. I embarked on a crash course to supplement my schoolboy French. I think was just about the funniest hour of my life. There was great hilarity which probably masked our nervousness. When it came to it I stumbled through it well enough."

If that sounded somewhat amateurish, there appeared more than enough substance and style in the presentation to back up the positive report from the Executive Board. But no-one in the golf camp viewed acceptance as a gimme. "We had to wait a few hours and that was a pretty tense period," Dawson remembered.

The result was as hoped for and, frankly, as expected. Rugby sevens, which had been campaigning for many years, was accepted by 81 votes to 8, a decision which, as it transpired, gave poignancy to the words of legendary All Black winger Jonah Lomu. When quizzed by a delegate at an earlier presentation about what rugby would prefer in a venue Lomu declared in that disarmingly laid-back manner of his: "Just say where you are and we'll be there." Sadly, the always popular Lomu, whose untimely death at the age of 40 in November, 2015 was mourned by the sporting world, will not be there.

The vote in favour of golf was 63-27, adequate rather than spectacular. Two people in the auditorium that day had reason to celebrate more than most, the two people from the world of amateur golf in countries less steeped in the history of the game who more than any probably battered the conservative defences of golf into eventual submission. Stand up Emma Villacieros and Claude-Roger Cartier, the presidents of respectively the Spanish and French golf federations. In the case of Villacieros, she stood up on witnessing the decision in the auditorium and jumped about like a Spanish flea. Others were more restrained.

"I am a sitter and nodder," Dawson said.

Billy Payne, who had been forced to abort attempts to get golf into the Atlanta Olympics, was delighted with the outcome from both a personal viewpoint and as chairman of Augusta National. "I think it is maybe the best thing for the game of golf in terms of its worldwide growth that's happened in the last 50 years," Payne stated. "I'm just thrilled because my experience has been that once something as important as an Olympic medal is available, those countries who consider their Olympic participation as an extension of their nationalism, of their pride, of their growth, they're going to say: 'Well here's another medal available, let's go get it.' As Asia continues to grow, and as golf grows in South America – it'll get a definite kick from the first one being there, I suspect – give it a decade, and you'll be able to measure the impact that the Olympics had on growth of participation."

Ken Schofield, who was one of those officials to receive regular ear-bashings from Villacieros, is similarly optimistic while also cautious about where and when the effects will be seen. "(The Olympics) probably will help participation, maybe not immediately and not in our markets. We have seen a stagnation here after a period of tremendous growth. There is a different culture and people are less prepared to spend half a day playing golf and socialising in the clubhouse afterwards. However, I don't see the game in crisis and the Olympics will help. Great Britain & Ireland should have a good chance of medals."

The decision taken, there was much to do. The following year saw golf and rugby attend an orientation ceremony in Lausanne. The IGF decided to open an office in the Maison du Sport in Lausanne headed by its executive director, Antony Scanlon. The Australian had been working full-time for the IOC as Head of Games Co-ordination, Operations and Services having previously been involved in various capacities on the organising committees

175

of the Sydney, Salt Lake City and Athens Olympics. An Athletes Committee comprising 22 professional golfers from around the world was established. There was, too, the London Olympics to study in all its aspects, from transport to ticketing.

But one thing above all dominated thinking and caused concern in the wake of the announcement in Copenhagen in October, 2009. And it emanated from a decision taken a week earlier at the same IOC session.

16

PICKING WEEDS BY HAND

Golf was in the same situation as rugby, on behalf of whom Jonah Lomu had said: "Just say where you are and we'll be there." Both had prepared their bids blind in the sense that the decision on the venue would not be known until a week prior to the announcement of the newly admitted sports. Like Forrest Gump's box of chocolates, they did not know what they were 'gonna git.' There were four contenders.

Would it be Chicago, the city that built America's first 18-hole course and a hotbed of enthusiastic golf fans? Would it be Madrid, home to the excellent Club de Campo Villa, a course part designed by Seve Ballesteros, one of the earliest campaigners for golf in the Olympics? Would it be Tokyo in golf-mad Japan with its 2,349 courses (and counting) and many more driving ranges? Or would it be Rio de Janeiro with its monoculture of football and barely a whiff of golfing heritage? There would be more people on the Copacabana Beach on a rainy Monday than golfers in the city.

The votes were counted. Chicago, helped or hindered by the speech of Barack Obama (the outcome suggests the latter), dropped out in the first round with 18 votes, four behind Tokyo, with Madrid on 28, marginally ahead of Rio's 26. Tokyo was next for the axe with 20 votes, leaving Rio to overcome Madrid in the final round by 66 to 32.

Golf was going to have to make its crucial first appearance –

officially, that is – at the Olympics for 112 years in a country with just 25,000 golfers out of a population of 209 million serviced by around 100 golf courses. The comparison is perhaps a little unfair but Scotland, with a population of 5.3 million boasts just under 600 courses. Little wonder that the words poisoned chalice were whispered in the corridor of powers.

Schofield, speaking with the freedom of a former official, looks back in disappointment. "We did all that work and got the worst of all the possible venues," he said. "If we pass reasonable muster there, a much bigger opportunity presents itself in Tokyo in 2020. After that it might be Paris with tennis at probably Roland Garos and golf at Le Golf National where the Ryder Cup will be held in 2018."

Dawson was more diplomatic. "From a golf point of view, Rio was the most difficult," he admitted.

Just how difficult became all too apparent on the first visit of IGF officials to Rio de Janeiro. A tour of the possible courses in the Rio area demonstrated with little need for consideration that none was of sufficient quality to provide a decent test for the modern professional. The decision was taken to find a suitable site and build a new course.

Easier said than done, only the more so in a country where golf is played by not much more than a handful of wealthy businessmen. People invariably object to development and they have every right to do so. When that development is for a land-devouring, water-guzzling golf course in a country where the population neither cares about nor understands what to them amounts to elitist recreation the dissent is going to be louder. And when it is for such a gigantic, easy-to-hit target as the Olympic Games then the noise will reach fever pitch.

A bumpy journey was expected; a turbulent roller coaster ride with few highs was delivered. The chosen site at Reserva de Marapendi in the wealthy Barra da Tijuca district, an area of gated communities and high end, high rise, high price buildings and the home for many of the Olympic venues, proved controversial for a number of reasons.

It was, according to environmentalists, a nature reserve, a wetland, a home for cuddly little alligators, namely broad-snooted caimans, less cute capybaras and snakes, birds and the Fluminense swallowtail butterfly. 'Occupy Golf', a small but voluble group, let their presence be known, even if it was not exactly 'Occupy Wall Street'.

Nonsense, the Municipal Olympic Committee told protesters, the chosen area was empty and abandoned, a home to an illegal operation dredging sand for concrete.

There were legal arguments about the ownership of the property, legal arguments about the development, legal arguments about whether environmental regulations were being followed and legal arguments about the legal arguments. There was, consequently, delay after delay after delay.

At the heart of the controversy were Eduardo Paez, the mayor of Rio, and Pasquale Mauro, an 84-year-old Italian-born billionaire property developer who provided finance and will no doubt get his reward not in heaven but in 23 luxury condominiums rising 22 storeys in that general direction.

The Rio Organising Committee had chosen in March 2012 highly respected American golf architect Gil Hanse to design the new course, close to, though not directly bordering, the ocean and about two miles from the Olympic Village. Hanse had been riding a wave of adulation for his work on the new links at Castle Stuart in Inverness, his remodelling of TPC Boston and his refashioning of the Blue Monster at Doral. The committee had considered eight bids, including one each from the so-called Big Three – Jack Nicklaus, Arnold Palmer and Gary Player – and a big fourth in Greg Norman. It was suggested that Hanse's willingness to be hands-on down in Rio and his sympathetic approach towards local vegetation and natural contours proved decisive.

Four years after golf was readmitted to the Olympics, the permissions were finalised and construction could begin. "We have been trying to make up time ever since," Dawson admitted.

Not that the green light for work to start meant an end to the delays. The build itself and the maintenance were fraught with difficulties, not least because the local workforce had little, if any, experience of creating a golf course and local businesses did not stock the necessary equipment. Everything had to be imported.

Londoner Neil Cleverly, who has become known as the Indiana Jones of golf course management during his adventurous 25 years in the business, has been the man at the centre of those problems since being appointed course superintendent in 2013.

"When I saw the equipment I had and the novice workforce I had, I thought, 'Oh my God, are we really going to do this?' he told *Pitchcare.com*, an industry website. "It has been insane. You have to embrace the culture around you. It is what you make it. You can't import Florida into Rio. It just doesn't work that way. You have to be resourceful. There is no outlet here where I can go to buy everyday golf course maintenance items. Everything has to come from overseas."

Cleverly, a former British military man, had tackled start-up courses in remote places like Egypt, Dominican Republic and Mexico. But he had never confronted anything like this. The resignation rate among the workforce, for example, rattled along at around 30% a month. Basically, one in three of his workers packed in every four weeks principally because they could not stand picking weeds by hand 24/7. The hand picking of weeds was a necessity due to the ban on herbicides. Yet, there was tremendous loyalty, too, among some of the manual labourers who travelled four hours by bus to work and four hours home again every day. Not that they had much choice.

Hanse admitted that during the darkest periods he allowed

thoughts of potential incompletion to penetrate his positive thinking. But they were only fleeting and not that serious. As he put it: "The project was too important not get finished. But it took twice as long as it should have taken to build it."

Every Olympics in recent memory, and beyond, have generated scare stories about venues not being ready, expensive tickets not being sold, rampant water pollution, air not fit to breathe, environmental catastrophe, wafer-thin security and so on. And pretty much every Games have played out in magnificent stadiums and arenas in front of full houses with the tales of impending doom evaporating in the heady atmosphere of great sporting endeavour and dodgy old national pride.

Of the six summer Olympics covered by the author only Atlanta in 1996 failed to receive the 'best ever' tag which the IOC president has traditionally granted the hosts at his closing ceremony speech. Deservedly so. The American organisers went to Barcelona, observed the unexpected brilliance of the Spanish arrangements and returned home to do their own thing. Not very well, as it happened.

Barcelona, Sydney, Athens, Beijing and London have all exceeded expectations and it would be pretty surprising if the carnival city of Rio de Janeiro, with a backdrop to die for, does not do the same. Being visually stunning has become so important in the television and tablet age and one can surely imagine there will be plenty pictures of golfers driving towards the hazy distant splendour of Christ The Redeemer. The statue, one of the seven modern wonders of the world, will take its place in Olympic imagery alongside the likes of the Sydney Harbour Bridge, The Parthenon, The Bird's Nest Stadium and Buckingham Palace.

As the Olympic year of 2016 arrived, initial reservation among professional golfers about the Olympic Games either vanished or went underground. Only the Australian Adam Scott of the leading players sounded a negative note with his description of the

Olympic tournament event as "an exhibition event" and his subsequent comment that "some time off looks quite good actually."

Scott told Reuters: "Whether I win an Olympic medal or not is not going to define my career or change whether I've fulfilled my career. For me, it's all about the four majors and I think that's the way it should stay for golf. Most of the athletes at the Olympics have probably trained four years specifically to peak at this one event. It's the pinnacle of their sport… (golf) doesn't need to be in the Olympics."

Otherwise, it has been a case of 'bring it on', from leading American Jordan Speith right down the rankings from which the players will be selected. There has been some disquiet among commentators about the fact that by limiting the fields to 60 men and 60 women and by restricting the number of players per country to four (if in the top 15 in world) or two, the quality of the entry will be compromised. This is particularly relevant to the women's tournament where South Korea provided 20 of the world top 50 when this was written. Only four of them would be allowed to compete.

But this is the Olympics, not an LPGA event. This is not unusual. One remembers Giles Scott winning both the 2011 European and World Championships in sailing's Finn Class yet failing to gain selection for the British team because of the presence of the incomparable, multi-gold medallist Ben Ainslie and only one spot available per country.

It is always important when the best in a sport gives his backing to a project. Speith was unequivocal in his support. "When I was really young, I always thought of the Olympians that walked in the opening ceremonies as the greatest-athletes-in-the-world type of thing," he said. "But once I chose golf, I didn't think it would ever be a reality. To be one of those athletes… I would never forget that ceremony and that walk, walking with the American flag… It would be awesome if I could make that team.

"Winning a gold medal has got to be up there now, in my mind, with winning a major championship. I've been asked the question: a Green Jacket or a gold medal? A Wannamaker Trophy (USP-GA Championship) or an Open Championship or a gold medal? That's not fair. I think this year we are going to approach it as a fifth major and we're going to prepare like it is. I'm going down there and try and take care of business. Staying in the village and doing whatever it is, meeting these incredible athletes from around the world, hopefully that's something I will be experiencing."

Fellow American Bubba Watson, who metaphorically (and sometimes literally) wears the stars and stripes on his sleeve, has gone further. "I would say it would be a little bit bigger than a Green Jacket. It's more rare. The game of golf hasn't seen it for years. And I get to keep that gold medal for life. I don't have to give it back after a year. How would you not want to be an Olympic athlete? My wife has qualified for the Olympics for basketball but was injured. So, she never got to play."

In fact, Toronto-born Angie Ball Watson, all 6ft 4inches of her, gained selection for the 2000 Canadian Olympic team only for one of the many injuries which blighted her career preventing her gaining any court time. The couple met at the University of Georgia where Ball played for the Lady Bulldogs on the way to a professional career, first in Italy and then back in the States in Charlotte, cut short by serious knee and cruciate problems.

The Olympic connection has also clearly played a factor in the enthusiasm displayed by Dustin Johnson, another American member of the world elite. DJ, as golf knows him, is engaged to Paulina Gretsky, the daughter of Canadian ice hockey legend Wayne, aka, modesty apart, The Great One. "Obviously, I've talked to Wayne and he said it's really cool," Johnson said. "The thing I would look forward most to would be just walking in the opening ceremony. I think it would be awesome."

The Olympic flame burns just as brightly in the home of

Justin Rose, England's highest ranked player at the time of writing. "For me it's a huge opportunity," Rose says. "My wife Kate is a former European champion gymnast in sports acrobatics which was never recognised (as an Olympic sport). But she hoped one day it would be, so the Olympics for her was always a dream and a goal. In my house it is a big deal and it's definitely a goal of mine to represent Team GB and go there and win a medal."

European Tour golfers from the Continent have always been pro-Olympics. No less so – perhaps even more so – the Scandanavians for whom the Winter Olympics would be the most important event in the sporting calendar. Henrik Stenson, who is likely to lead the Swedish team, is another looking forward to Rio. "I see it as a once-in-a-lifetime opportunity to be part of the Olympics," he said. "It's a cool event and, given my age (40), it could be the only chance I have. I think I'd stay in the village to get the feel of it. That would elevate the experience."

Scotland's Catriona Matthew will be challenging for one of the two spots available in the British team. Although not entirely convinced that golf is a perfect fit for the Olympics, she accepts what many in her sport believe, namely that "Olympic golf could become the biggest thing in the women's game." Matthew added: "And I'd certainly like to win a medal in it."

There is no such doubt in the young mind of Lydia Ko, the world No. 1, who will represent New Zealand as a 19-year-old in Brazil. "Ever since they announced that golf will be in the Olympics, I said, 'Hey, I want to get myself on that team.' For any athlete to say you're an Olympian is a whole new proud feeling, and to represent your country on such an international stage is going to be pretty special."

While some remain unhappy about the fairness of the qualification process, others have expressed disquiet about the absence of a team element and the fact that the individual medals will be determined by the routine four rounds of stroke play rather than the head-to-head of match play.

"It is not a team event, I think unfortunately," Speith, for one, remarked.

Olympic rules actually forbid team events that are merely add-ons to individual competition. Stroke play, meanwhile, was very much the preferred option of the players themselves who were quizzed by the International Golf Federation about how they would want the event to be decided. The IGF told the IOC: "Golf's top athletes prefer four rounds of stroke play because they feel it is the fairest and best way of identifying a champion. The IGF and the top players feel the format would place golf in the Olympic Games on a level with the sport's major championships, all of which share the stroke play format and are historically accepted as the ultimate indicator of an athlete's success in the sport."

That said, both the IGF and the IOC in the considerable shape of its president Thomas Bach would be prepared to reassess that format in the wake of Rio. Bach said on the subject, "If we think match play would be more interesting then the format we are going to have now, then we can still change for the Olympic Games in Tokyo."

And after Tokyo in 2020 comes the review which will determine the future of golf as an Olympic sport.

It would be a surprise if it did not become as permanent a feature as tennis given that the vast majority of the best players in the world seem eager for the experience. That, in turn, should generate top class competition and complete the two most important factors in the assessment process.

That has already been spelled out by Bach. "It's about having the best players in the world and the great competition, and then seeing how attractive the golf tournament is on a worldwide scale," he said. "This will be… a new experience for golf, to see how it does among all the other 28 sports in the Olympic programme, so not to be on a stand-alone basis any more but being in the middle of a multi-sport event and having to find its role. But I'm very sure that golf will find its place.

"The Olympic Games are about the best athletes in the world coming together. Of course, it would help golf to get good worldwide distribution and also ranking because for golf and the International Federation it is a unique opportunity to promote golf on a real worldwide scale. You will have golf in more than 200 countries in the world, in every country in the world. You will have billions of TV viewers and therefore I would think it would be good if you have not only as many players from as many different national Olympic committees being qualified but also a broad distribution of medals and rankings."

There is every chance of that. A quick perusal of the world golf rankings suggested to this eye a decent chance of 10 countries being legitimate challengers for a medal, and you could not say that of many, if any, of the other 27 sports. There were perhaps as many as 50 golfers who could win any given major championship, and that certainly could not be said of, for example, tennis.

Any of the four American golfers in the field, most prominently Jordan Speith, was a possible medallist. Continue down the list: Jason Day (and Adam Scott, if he does not go on holiday) for Australia; Rory McIlroy and even Shane Lowry for Ireland; Henrik Stenson representing Sweden, Great Britain's Justin Rose and whoever joins him, maybe Danny Willet, maybe Andy Sullivan; Louis Oosthuizen and Branden Grace of South Africa; Sergio Garcia, by no means past it yet, for Spain; Japan's Hideki Matsuyama around whom his country's media interest will be huge; Martin Kaymer for Germany; and, should he begin to fulfil his immense promise, the French enigma that is Victor Dubuisson. That could be a conservative assessment.

The point about the size of the television audience and its benefit to the growth of golf was taken up by Rory McIlroy,

186

one of the favourites for the gold medal. "It puts our sport on a bigger stage," he said. "People who do not necessarily watch golf are going to watch because it is the Olympics."

There is one element of the Olympics that the pampered jet-setters of the golfing world will not be enjoying – the so-called 'whereabouts rule' by which all the Olympic golfers, both male and female, are required to inform anti-doping officials where they are going to be for one hour each day between 5am and 11pm. This out-of-competition targeted blood testing, due to commence 13 weeks prior to the start of the Games, is not something golfers have been used to. Not a problem, surely, since all they need to tell authorities is whatever practice range they happen to be using on any particular day. The practice range is the golfer's default home from home.

"The athletes will have to accept the Olympic standards during the year prior to the Games and, of course, during the Games the first five will be tested on top of the random-testing and the targeted-testing during the Olympic period," Bach explained.

For its part, Olympic Golf commits to operating, according to a statement in 2015, "under the IGF's anti-doping policy which is WADA (World Anti-Doping Agency) compliant... From May 6 through to the conclusion of the Olympic Games there will be a registered testing pool, created and managed by the IGF, and male and female golfing athletes will be subject to both urine and blood tests for substances on the WADA prohibited list."

The PGA Tour in America, unlike the European Tour, however, is still sticking with its own WADA-lite doping policy. WADA says the Tour needs to make three changes in order to comply fully with the WADA code - adopt the full prohibited list, establish a more rigorous method of out-of-competition testing and reform the 'secret' process by which sanctions are handed out.

Bach made his point without coming on too strong. "I can only encourage the PGA Tour to follow and finally accept the

WADA code and to be compliant with this so that you have a harmonised anti-doping regime there for all the golf players and that you have an equal level of playing field for all the golfers," he said during the 2015 Open at St Andrews.

Peter Dawson says that even before a ball has been struck in Rio there are signs of an upsurge in interest in golf and of governments providing finance for the sport. "I will give you one example," the International Golf Federation official said. "Out of the blue, the Argentina government is funding Argentinian teams to go round South America playing matches."

It is reckoned that under-resourced women's golf will benefit the most. For is not an Olympic gold medal an Olympic gold medal? There is no distinction made between male golds and female golds.

17

OUR 'ENRY'S BELT AND HITLER'S TROPHY

O f the 410 lots in the glossy Bonhams catalogue for its 2012 spring Sporting & Golfing Memorabilia Auction, three in particular commanded worldwide interest.

The front cover highlighted the central oval enamel portrait of Lord Lonsdale on the Gold Heavyweight belt won by Henry Cooper twice in 1959 and again in 1961; inside the brochure there was a photograph of a somewhat battered red cricket ball – accompanied by a signed letter of apparent authenticity – which had been smote to all parts of the St Helens Ground, Swansea, by Gary Sobers in his historic six sixes in one over in 1968; and on the inside front cover was the unique amber and gold golfing oddity which became known as The Hitler Trophy.

'Our 'Enry', as Sir Henry Cooper was affectionately known by an adoring British public, had died a year earlier at the age of 76. The Lonsdale Belt, the first of three won by the Londoner during his 17-year career, had been previously sold at auction for £42,000 in 1993, a sale prompted by his heavy losses on the Lloyd's Insurance market.

The guide price in the Chester showroom that May day was £40,000 to £60,000. Boxing memorabilia had been growing in popularity. Just a few months earlier the famous blood-red velvet trunks worn by Muhammad Ali during his 1971 defeat by Joe Frazier – a genuine 'Fight of the Century' also known as simply 'The Fight' – fetched a world record £115,000 at auction.

Bidding for the Lonsdale Belt, according to a contemporary report, was "competitive" before the hammer came down at a price of £49,250. Once more the belt, inscribed as the "sole property of Henry Cooper who has won the heavyweight championship of Great Britain three times", was on the move.

There has been much more controversy about the movements, or not, of the ball, or not, used the day poor Malcolm Nash, the Glamorgan medium pace bowler, received the full treatment at the hands of the incomparable Sir Garfield Sobers. The row, which has raged ever since the ball was auctioned by Christie's in 2006, spawned a book called Howzat? The Six Sixes Ball Mystery written by journalist and author Grahame Lloyd whose investigations turned into a later life's work.

Cricket fans and, indeed, all sports enthusiasts of a certain age, will remember the grainy black and white BBC film of the 32-year-old West Indies and Nottinghamshire captain belting the ball over the boundary and, in the case of the final ball of the over, out of the ground. The ball was retrieved from a garden by a young lad named Richard Lewis who was photographed presenting it to Sobers. Sobers later handed a ball to John Gough, the then secretary of the Nottingham Supporters' Association, only for him subsequently to pass it on to another secretary, Jose Miller.

"The most likely theory – and the one I favour – is that Sobers pulled the wrong ball out of his cricket bag and handed over one of the Dukes used by Nottinghamshire," Lloyd said. A simple mistake, it seems.

Decades later, in need of funds, Jose Miller put the Duke & Son ball in her possession up for sale at Christie's, who obtained a letter of authenticity hand signed by the cricketing knight. It read: "I, Sir Garfield Sobers, confirm that this signed cricket ball was bowled during the over in which I hit six sixes off Malcolm Nash in the County Championship Match at the St Helens Ground, Swansea in 1968 between Glamorgan and Nottinghamshire." It made £26,400 at auction in 2006.

Even at that stage there were serious doubts about the validity of the ball, albeit never with any accompanying suggestion of impropriety on the part of Sobers, who did not gain financially from the sale. Nash, the unfortunate bowler, who Christie's never contacted at any stage, insisted that the ball he used for that fateful over - the same make used in every match by Glamorgan – was not a Dukes but a Surridge. Television evidence seems to endorse a view shared by Lloyd as a result of his extensive investigations and interviews with old players and officials. The sale proceeded, however, and ever since Christie's have played a straight bat towards all doubting deliveries, maintaining their signed certificate represented "good provenance".

The item was shipped to India. But the buyer, described as an Indian art impressario, failed to pay import duty charges at New Delhi Airport. That led to the ball being sold again via e-auction. The next chapter of the story saw Bonhams planning to auction the Six Sixes cricket ball in Chester on May 29. But they decided to withdraw Lot 32, stating the existence of "compelling and conclusive" evidence that cast a doubt on authenticity.

Nash, meanwhile, back in Wales after years in North America, remains distressed at what he considers an attack on his integrity. "I'm still amazed why anyone would want to dispute the fact that we used a Surridge ball," he insists.

Two 'mysteries' in one auction certainly spelled coincidence. Although no-one had ever cast doubt on the origin of The Hitler Trophy, there was that lengthy period when its whereabouts were known by only a handful of people. There was, too, the Anglo-German debate over whether or not Hitler turned back on his way to the prize-giving, unable to countenance presenting his trophy to a couple of Englishmen.

In the early months of 2012, as the Rio 2016 Committee were preparing to award the design contract for the Olympic golf course to Gil Hanse, Bonhams were gathering together the lots for their May auction and preparing the catalogue for distribution. There would be sections covering cricket, golf, boxing and football.

The highest estimate price among the football memorabilia of £6,000-8,000 was for the 1956 FA Cup Winners Medal presented to Dave Ewing, Manchester City's Scottish centre half. City defeated by three goals to one a Birmingham City team which at the time had become the first to reach the FA Cup final without playing at home. The match is mostly remembered for the goalkeeping heroics of Bert Trautmann who continued playing despite breaking a bone in his neck in a collision with Birmingham's Peter Murphy with 17 minutes of the Final remaining.

A Pele limited edition Gloria Book (Carnival edition No 0006 of 2,500) in its original presentation box, accompanied by a colour print hand signed by all the surviving members of the three time World Cup-winning 1970 Brazil team, had an asking price of £5,000 to £6,000.

But Derek Holden and Julien McEnery, the Hesketh secretary, were focussed only on Lot 169, "A large 1936 silver-gilt 'Grosser Golfpreis' '", as the catalogue described it, with a vague estimate of £10,000 to £20,000 reflecting the uncertainty of the auctioneers over the unusual and unique nature of the trophy.

Cricket was first up and quickly over. There were only 32 Lots, the last the withdrawn Six Sixes ball. A folder of around 20 Australian signed team sheets, covering a period from 1899 to 1993, with an estimate of £800 to £1,000 sold for £2,700; a collection of 1890s to 1960s letters from 'cricket gentlemen' like Wally Hammond and Pelham Warner, including correspondence with Chequers and Downing Street, went for £3,600, six times the estimate; the hammer came down on a G G Hearne cricket bat from the early 1900s, featuring 83 signatures headed by W G Grace, at £3,700. Prices were good.

Golfing Memorabilia, Lots 33-252, comprised the bulk of the auction. It covered autographs, balls, books, ceramics, paintings and prints, medals and badges, clubs and trophies. A John C Gourlay feather golf ball dating from the mid-1800s sold for £4,000 while a First Edition Wethered and Simpson: *The Architectural Side of Golf* went for a chunky yet disappointing £3,200.

But the undoubted star of the show was The Hitler Trophy.

Holden and McEnery had travelled separately from Hesketh to Chester, each accompanied by a friend. Their different arrival times explained why McEnery was seated in the packed body of the kirk, as it were, and Holden was stationed at the back. McEnery, clutching a numbered card in understandably sweaty hands, was trusted with the bidding. He had £20,000 in the kitty with the latitude to go slightly higher if required. Like an expectant father, Holden assumed the role of nervous observer.

The sight of a Ganton representative among the 100 or so in the room worried Holden for a moment. Ganton was a wealthy club who had members easily able to put up the money for the trophy. The motorway meeting had not been entirely cordial. Was Ganton going to try to buy the trophy after all?

"I went just out of interest," Ian Douglas explained. "We never had any intention of bidding."

Unbeknown to Holden, though not to Bonhams, there was at least one other intended bidder in the room. Christoph Meister, liaison officer with the German Golf Association and an honorary delegate of the German Golf Archive as well as the noted co-author of a history of German golf, was in attendance on behalf of the former. The German valuation of the trophy was £10,000 to 12,000. He was armed with funds to match the upper figure, and no more.

As Kuno Schuch, director of the German Golf Archives, stated: "The German Golf Association were not publicly enthusiastic about obtaining the trophy. So, the money was not from the official funds of the association. It was provided by three private individuals and we did not really think it would be enough."

Perhaps that was why, again unbeknown to the Hesketh delegation, Meister took photographs of the trophy inside the glass case in the showroom on the morning prior to the event and persuaded one of the auction house employees to take his picture holding the trophy. He clearly did not expect to be taking it with him back to Germany.

"Lot 169," the auctioneer announced before describing the trophy in detail. A hush had fallen over the room.

Bidding began with the Hesketh treasurer holding up his card at £9,000. The auctioneer announced a commission bid of £9,500.

Holden was disappointed but not surprised. "We wondered who it was. It was a pity that someone else was bidding but we had pretty much expected that."

In fact, Holden left that day convinced that the commission bids left on the book in advance had belonged to the German Golf Association. Both contemporary and subsequent reports to this day have all assumed that the undeclared bidder was the German Golf Association. Although the German Golf Association might still have been wary about coveting a trophy bearing the name of Adolf Hitler, the climate had changed sufficiently for many in Germany to appreciate the historic nature and desire its return home.

"It wasn't me," Meister insisted. "I never made a bid. I ran out of money pretty quickly."

McEnery, perhaps unsettled by the commission bid, was worryingly slow to resume the bidding at £10,000, at least in the mind's eye of an anxious Holden. But the treasurer raised his card in time.

The bidding now continued apace – £10,500 on the book, £11,000 Hesketh; £11,500 on the book, £12,000 Hesketh; £12,500 on the book, £13,000 Hesketh; £13,500 on the book, £14,000

Hesketh; £14,500 on the book…

Holden thought: "This is getting close. I knew the VAT would be taking the amount near to our limit. I did not want to lose it. I was thinking about the need to chip in myself. I was very determined. As I said, not obsessive, just passionate. Some in the golf club were fed up hearing about it. Others were very much in favour of what we were trying to do. That's what golf clubs are like. Always politics."

Hesketh were not done yet. "£15,000," the auctioneer called out. McEnery lifted his card. "That's me out," the auctioneer declared, indicating he had reached the limit of the commission bid.

"£15,500 once, £15,500 twice," and, with no-one twitching, the hammer fell. Cue applause.

There was no late intervention from Ganton. The man from the German Golf Association, still anonymous to all but the Bonham's staff, neither uttered a word nor moved a muscle. There were no other bids. Hesketh had got their man's trophy and within budget at £15,000 plus VAT.

"I was relieved and elated," Holden recalled. "I know that Arnold (Bentley) would have been the first to downplay his role in the tournament, but I believe it would have pleased him to know that the trophy would wind up where it belonged. He had died, after all, not even knowing where it was."

There was also a fair measure of pleasure at the outcome from perhaps a suprising source. Kuno Schuch, who would have been delighted to welcome the Grosser Golfpreis in the German Golf Archives, could not have taken defeat with greater grace.

"It is a unique prize, well designed and produced," he commented. "The material has its value. But it is the history that makes it unique. I am glad it is at Hesketh Golf Club and not in a private collection of a collector of Third Reich material and trophies. I'm really happy that is open to the public and not locked away."

Schuch had hinted on the very real possibility of the under-

195

bidder being a collector of Nazi memorabilia and that The Hitler Trophy could have been lost into a private stash of SS uniforms, swastika flags and the like. Meister thinks that the likeliest candidate, given the modest size of the market in Germany, was an American golf collector. Golf items represent huge business in the States.

It is understood that the R&A and its British Golf Museum were not involved. We shall never know the answer to the mystery. It is standard practice for auctioneers to preserve the anonymity in such instances and, true to that, Bonhams will not reveal the identity of the underbidder.

Hesketh did not care. McEnery picked up the trophy, now packed safely in its rather dusty black box, stuck it in his boot and drove home.

"It stayed in his house for a while," Holden remembered. "Julien's wife said immediately that it needed cleaning. We arranged for a retired jeweller neighbour of mine to clean it professionally. It looked a bit tarnished at the edges. It was three or four weeks before it appeared in the clubhouse. The membership seemed thrilled and delighted. Of course, there were a few mutterings about why we were providing a home to something associated with Adolf Hitler.

"The unveiling took place prior to the July Club Dinner. There was quite a gathering as we exhibited the trophy in a specially commissioned cabinet with appropriate security systems. It was typical of the generosity of some that on seeing the cabinet a member asked me to send him the invoice and he would take care of it.

"We have always tried to call it the Golf Prize of Nations. But a newspaper christened it The Hitler Trophy and the name has well and truly stuck. Everyone now refers to it as The Hitler Trophy."

Bob Bentley, appropriately enough, was invited to say a few words. "I wish more of my father's friends were still around to witness the occasion and to see this wonderful trophy here at

Hesketh, where I feel it should have been long before now."

Derek Holden, without whose sterling efforts the trophy might have 'disappeared' for a second time in its winding history, acknowledged the contribution of the members who donated to the appeal fund. Past captains, in fact, provided 60% of the donations, each stumping up a four-figure amount.

"It was always a disappointment to Arnold, and to Robert, that due to a series of unusual circumstances he was denied the opportunity of bringing the trophy to Hesketh," Holden told the assembled gathering. "I am proud to have been partly responsible for remedying that situation."

Originally situated in its cabinet to the right of the bar in the main lounge, it quickly became a fascinating attraction for all visitors. They could study it up close, turn round to look out of the window at The Hitler Tree and marvel at a curious link that spanned in the Olympic year of 2016 eight decades and two nations who fought two of the bloodiest wars in history.

Logically, though, the more obvious resting place for the trophy was in the Bentley Room which, located on the other side of the splendid old clubhouse, contains other Baden-Baden mementoes as well as trophies, medals and photographs relating to both Bentley brothers as well as their father, Hesketh stalwarts all. Now, after a recent complete renovation and construction of a patio in the Bentley Room, the trophy has assumed a central focal point there in between portraits of the two brothers.

That should prove its final resting place. After all, it moved around enough in its time. There it will remain, other than the occasional day out to a local Rotary Club meeting or some such function.

The odd golfing VIP has already been known to drop by. There was, for example, a delegation from the Professional Golf Association of America, headed by the then president Ted Bishop and accompanied by his vice-president Derek Sprague. Little did anyone know at the time, as photographs were taken of the pair with the trophy, that Bishop was soon to be replaced by his deputy following an incident involving English Ryder Cup player Ian Poulter.

Bishop reacted to criticism of Nick Faldo in Poulter's book *No Limits* by tweeting the comment 'Yours or His? Lil Girl' in relation to Poulter's greatly inferior record. The PGA of America swiftly removed Bishop, describing his statements - there were others on his Facebook page - as "unacceptable" and "insensitive" and "gender-based".

The Olympic year of 2016 had only just begun when Hesketh were contacted by someone offering the Lancashire club a medal from 1936. It was inscribed 'Olympiade Jahr 1936 Deutscher Golf Verband' on on side and on the reverse the words 'As a Memento of the first meeting between the English Golf Union and the Deutsche Golf Verband'. The price was agreed at £350 and Hesketh became the proud owners of another piece of history from the Baden-Baden event.

The seller was a Scottish professional golfer by the name of Andrew Gauld, based in Germany. Gauld maintained a measured vagueness to both the club and the author about the medal's acquisition. He said only that he obtained it in England, though it remains unclear whether at auction or not. References to 'The Major' suggest that the medal had belonged to Tiny Lavarack, the former secretary of the English Golf Union. We know for certain that Lavarack was in Baden-Baden for the tournament and as the highest ranking English golf official present would have been the person to whom the German Golf Association would present a medal and/or gift.

"It was probably in the hand of The Major until he died," Gauld said. "The person I got it from could only tell me that it belonged to his uncle at one stage. I was told by a historian that the medal was originally given to Major Tiny Lavarack of the EGU."

Holden confirmed that Hesketh's questioning of Gauld over the medal's background yielded little information. However, a little light came from within as Holden unearthed a reference to the medal in one of Arnold Bentley's newspaper clippings.

"We found a clipping from 1992 in which Ian Erskine, another former secretary of the EGU, told the journalist that he had for years rested his coffee cup on the medal on his desk in his office at the EGU."

Just as Glen Echo Golf Club in St Louis markets itself as an Olympic venue, Hesketh actively promotes its link with the Games. The club's 2016 Handbook features on the cover a photograph of The Hitler Trophy. "Hesketh Golf Club has a close affinity with golf at the Olympic Games," the booklet states. "...The Hitler Tree still flourishes on a sandhill beside the flagpole where it was planted during World War II... (There will probably be) more high profile visitors from golfing dignitaries in 2017 when the Open Championship returns to (nearby) Royal Birkdale."

18

SWITHERING NO MORE

We live in the age of opinion and not even considered opinion. We live at a time when instant opinion can have more currency than thoughtful judgement.

Everything has to be black or white and immediate. Grey areas are treated as exclusion zones. There is no room for one shade of grey, never mind 50. You can be black one day, white the next and no one is going to blame you for changing your mind providing you state your point of view with utter conviction.

But what if the evidence is genuinely conflicting, leading you in one direction then dragging you back towards the opposite? What if logic and common sense demand one view only for, simultaneously, word of mouth and hearsay to insist on an opposing one?

A jury might understand the difficulty but fence-sitting is not allowed in the court of public opinion. So, just what is the truth behind the story of Adolf Hitler's aborted journey to Baden-Baden?

There is surely no way that Hitler embarked on a 1,000-mile round trip by car from Berlin- or 600-mile from Berchtesgaden – to Baden-Baden on the chance of presenting a trophy to a couple of golfers when he had surely just had his fill of sport during two weeks plus of the Olympic Games.

And yet three Englishmen, independent of each other – Derek Holden and Bobby Bentley, respectively the friend and son of Arnold Bentley, and Geoffrey Cousins, a respected journalist –

were told that it did indeed happen. Holden and Bobby Bentley heard the story from Arnold Bentley, one of the victorious English players, while 30 years earlier Cousins heard the same tale from English Golf Union secretary Major Tiny Lavarack, who was present in Baden-Baden.

The logistics of the journey, on 1930s roads not the Autobahns of today, and without modern communication, cast extreme doubt over the German Chancellor taking off for Baden-Baden at short notice and, somehow, being stopped on the road by his British Ambassador in waiting Joachim von Ribbentrop. Clearly the stuff of fantasy.

And yet the English version of events, each one consistent with the others, say this is precisely what happened right down to the Führer's rage before ordering his driver to turn round.

Nowhere in the National Archives in Berlin, the archives in Munich, and also the records kept in the Museum in Baden-Baden, is there documentary proof of Hitler embarking on such a journey. The diary of his secretary makes no mention of any trip to the spa town.

And still Geoffrey Cousins wrote an article in 1955 for *The Star*, the now defunct London evening newspaper, retelling the story of England's victory in the Grand Prize of Nations and of how a Hitler on his way to present his trophy to a pair of German heroes headed home in the huff on being told of their change in fortunes.

Germany does not believe the story; England does. It should be decided by penalties...

A few years ago when Tiger Woods was in his pomp, your author asked the then World No. 1 at a press conference whether he had been "swithering" over a particular decision.

Woods looked bemused. "Swithering?" he asked.

I whispered to my colleague on my right. "Is that a Scottish word?" I asked.

201

"Yes, you idiot," came the reply. "He doesn't know what you are talking about."

Woods, having been made aware of the meaning, seemed delighted with the quaint word. I like to imagine him these days having a beer in the locker room after a round with his mates talking about how he had been swithering between a 7-iron and an 8-iron for his approach to a green.

Swithering, for those readers unfamiliar with the word, involves doubt, hesitation and uncertainty. One source gives a definition of being "unable to decide between two options".

That was how I was using it when quizzing Tiger Woods and that is how I have been feeling while researching and writing *The Hitler Trophy*. I have been swithering.

There was plenty of contemporary documentary evidence about Peggy Abbott going to her grave without knowing she had won the Olympic golf tournament in 1900; about George Lyon emerging unknown from Canada to whip the Americans in St Louis in 1904; about how a trophy was won then given away then lost; about how golf, after decades of resistance and rancour, finally got its act together to regain a place on the Olympic schedule.

We know for certain that the Olympic men's golf champion in 2016 will be the first not to wear a tie and that the Olympic women's champion will be the first not to wear a long skirt and petticoats.

We do not know for sure, however, the truth about Hitler's intention regarding the presentation of his trophy. It remains a mystery, some would argue a myth. It has always bothered the author, for example, that not one shred of evidence from a German source exists in relation to the car journey.

Until now.

It had proved exceedingly difficult to find out much about the two German players, Leonard von Beckerath and C A Hellmers.

Even the German Golf Archives could provide little more than dates of birth and death and their domestic triumphs and international appearances. Repeated approaches to the Beckeraths via a family website yielded nothing.

Suddenly, out of the blue and late in proceedings, there came a reply from Aurel von Beckerath, Leonard's son. Aurel von Beckerath still lives in Krefeld and is recognised as the last of the Memmonite silk barons. He runs not so much a factory as a small workshop making silk fabrics for ties and suits, employing just a handful of people.

I had asked him in general terms about his father and about the 1936 tournament without any reference to Hitler and the aborted car journey.

"Let me tell you first about a good golf story," he wrote in faltering English which, after further communication between us, I have modified to give meaning to his words. "Leo started the tournament at Baden-Baden in 1936 well but the situation changed. At the time the driver of AH (Adolf Hitler) was on his way to drive his boss to Baden-Baden. Once AH heard how my father got on he instructed the driver to turn the car round and head back.

"This story was told to me by Herr Wolfgang Egeler, the father-in-law of my sister, a teammate of my father's at Linn (Krefelder Golf Club where Beckerath was a member) in 1953."

Aurel von Beckerath heard nothing about the event directly from his father in the same way that the sons of both Arnold Bentley and Peter Thirsk were told little or nothing by their fathers. It was a period about which that generation did not wish to speak. It was just too painful.

But here was a German confirming to another German a story which was supposed to have been a British invention. Surely this was evidence to end swithering once and for all?

'SO HITLER WENT OFF IN THE HUFF' after all, as that *Sunday Post* headline stated in 1986...

ACKNOWLEDGEMENTS

Much help is required to bring a real-life story together, especially when all the eyewitnesses are dead, contemporary reports are scarce and sketchy and the subject matter, for some, is best forgotten.

Friends and family become valuable, pretty much essential, sources of information. Even then, when war and infamy are involved, descendants can remain as much in the dark as anyone else due to the reluctance of participants to talk.

So it has been with the tale of The Hitler Trophy, an obvious nickname for a highly unusual and unlikely piece of sporting silverware. Nevertheless, I have received a great deal of assistance, guidance, encouragement and suggestions in researching and writing this book.

I would like to thank the following: Derek Holden, for sharing his passion and readily providing access to his own research; Bob Bentley, for painting a colourful portrait of his father, Arnold, and his uncle, Harry; Nicky Helyer and Gilly Edwards, Tom Thirsk's granddaughters, and Mel Hutchinson, his great granddaughter, for opening up their memories and scrapbooks; Aurel von Beckerath, for his late, but very welcome, contribution about his father, Leonard; Peter Dawson, Ken Schofield and Sir Michael Bonallack, titans of golf administration all, for their invaluable insight; Leonard Sculthorp, for inviting me into his home and into his life's work; and Brian Prosser, for translating from German the meaning not just the words.

My trip to Germany was made all the more rewarding by the warm welcome and willing help of Kuno Schuch of the German Golf Archive in Cologne and Thomas Ihm who has lost more balls than he can count at his beloved Baden-Baden Golf Club. Christoph Meister, Dietrich Quanz and Wolfgang Scheffler also provided significant information.

I would also like to express my gratitude to Charlie Forbes Adam, Paul Corker, Ian Douglas, Craig Francis, Kevin Knox, Richard Penley-Martin, Anthony Robertson, Gordon Simpson, David Strang and Charlie Milne.

Ian Ridley, whose idea this was, proved the most encouraging publisher as well as a sympathetic and insightful editor. I would like to thank him and his daughter, Alex, who took some excellent contemporary photographs.

Finally, as is the tradition, and most importantly, my love to Morag, Kate and Patrick who remained loving and supportive to the grumpy old man in the study.

ALSO BY FLOODLIT DREAMS

ADDED TIME
Surviving Cancer, Death Threats and the Premier League
Mark Halsey with Ian Ridley
(Foreword by Jose Mourinho)

THE BOY IN BRAZIL
Living, Loving and Learning in the Land of Football
By Seth Burkett

A DAZZLING DARKNESS
The Darren Barker Story
Darren Barker with Ian Ridley

THE SOCCER SYNDROME
English Football's Golden Age
By John Moynihan
(Foreword by Patrick Barclay)

ABOUT THE AUTHOR

ALAN FRASER has been one of Fleet Street's leading sports writers for many years, gracing the pages of *The Independent* and the *Daily Mail* among others. Golf has been a passion and a speciality. Alan has covered all four golf majors, including every Open Championship between 1978 and 2014. He also attended and reported on the last six summer Olympic Games at Barcelona, Atlanta, Sydney, Athens, Beijing and London.

ALSO BY ALAN FRASER

Sam: The Autobiography of Sam Torrance

Out of Bounds: Legendary Tales from the 19th Hole
Sam Torrance with Alan Fraser